New Product And Process Developm
Complete Self-Assessment Guide

The guidance in this Self-Assessment is based on New Product And Process Development best practices and standards in business process architecture, design and quality management. The guidance is also based on the professional judgment of the individual collaborators listed in the Acknowledgments.

Notice of rights

You are licensed to use the Self-Assessment contents in your presentations and materials for internal use and customers without asking us - we are here to help.

Trademarks

Table of Contents

About The Art of Service

The Art of Service, Business Process Architects since 2000, is dedicated to helping stakeholders achieve excellence.

Defining, designing, creating, and implementing a process to solve a stakeholders challenge or meet an objective is the most valuable role… In EVERY group, company, organization and department.

Unless you're talking a one-time, single-use project, there should be a process. Whether that process is managed and implemented by humans, AI, or a combination of the two, it needs to be designed by someone with a complex enough perspective to ask the right questions.

Someone capable of asking the right questions and step back and say, 'What are we really trying to accomplish here? And is there a different way to look at it?'

With The Art of Service's Standard Requirements Self-Assessments, we empower people who can do just that — whether their title is marketer, entrepreneur, manager, salesperson, consultant, Business Process Manager, executive assistant, IT Manager, CIO etc... —they are the people who rule the future. They are people who watch the process as it happens, and ask the right questions to make the process work better.

Contact us when you need any support with this Self-Assessment and any help with templates, blue-prints and examples of standard documents you might need:

http://theartofservice.com
service@theartofservice.com

Included Resources - how to access

Included with your purchase of the book is the New Product

And Process Development Self-Assessment Spreadsheet Dashboard which contains all questions and Self-Assessment areas and auto-generates insights, graphs, and project RACI planning - all with examples to get you started right away.

How? Simply send an email to
access@theartofservice.com
with this books' title in the subject to get the New Product And Process Development Self Assessment Tool right away.

You will receive the following contents with New and Updated specific criteria:

- The latest quick edition of the book in PDF

- The latest complete edition of the book in PDF, which criteria correspond to the criteria in...

- The Self-Assessment Excel Dashboard, and...

- Example pre-filled Self-Assessment Excel Dashboard to get familiar with results generation

- In-depth specific Checklists covering the topic

- Project management checklists and templates to assist with implementation

INCLUDES LIFETIME SELF ASSESSMENT UPDATES

Every self assessment comes with Lifetime Updates and Lifetime Free Updated Books. Lifetime Updates is an industry-first feature which allows you to receive verified self assessment updates, ensuring you always have the most accurate information at your fingertips.

Get it now- you will be glad you did - do it now, before you forget.

Send an email to **access@theartofservice.com** with this books' title in the subject to get the New Product And Process Development Self Assessment Tool right away.

Purpose of this Self-Assessment

This Self-Assessment has been developed to improve understanding of the requirements and elements of New Product And Process Development, based on best practices and standards in business process architecture, design and quality management.

It is designed to allow for a rapid Self-Assessment to determine how closely existing management practices and procedures correspond to the elements of the Self-Assessment.

The criteria of requirements and elements of New Product And Process Development have been rephrased in the format of a Self-Assessment questionnaire, with a seven-criterion scoring system, as explained in this document.

In this format, even with limited background knowledge of New Product And Process Development, a manager can quickly review existing operations to determine how they measure up to the standards. This in turn can serve as the starting point of a 'gap analysis' to identify management tools or system elements that might usefully be implemented in the organization to help improve overall performance.

How to use the Self-Assessment

On the following pages are a series of questions to identify to what extent your New Product And Process Development initiative is complete in comparison to the requirements set in standards.

To facilitate answering the questions, there is a space in front of each question to enter a score on a scale of '1' to '5'.

1 Strongly Disagree

2 Disagree

3 Neutral

4 Agree

5 Strongly Agree

Read the question and rate it with the following in front of mind:

'In my belief,
the answer to this question is clearly defined'.

There are two ways in which you can choose to interpret this statement;
1. how aware are you that the answer to the question is clearly defined
2. for more in-depth analysis you can choose to gather evidence and confirm the answer to the question. This obviously will take more time, most Self-Assessment users opt for the first way to interpret the question and dig deeper later on based on the outcome of the

overall Self-Assessment.

A score of '1' would mean that the answer is not clear at all, where a '5' would mean the answer is crystal clear and defined. Leave emtpy when the question is not applicable or you don't want to answer it, you can skip it without affecting your score. Write your score in the space provided.

After you have responded to all the appropriate statements in each section, compute your average score for that section, using the formula provided, and round to the nearest tenth. Then transfer to the corresponding spoke in the New Product And Process Development Scorecard on the second next page of the Self-Assessment.

Your completed New Product And Process Development Scorecard will give you a clear presentation of which New Product And Process Development areas need attention.

New Product And Process Development Scorecard Example

Example of how the finalized Scorecard can look like:

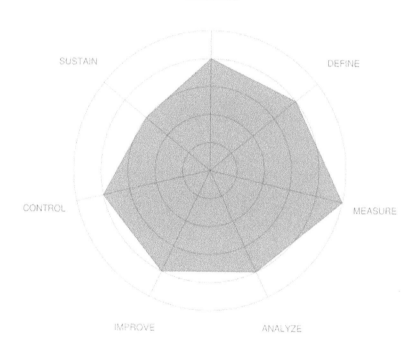

New Product And Process Development Scorecard

Your Scores:

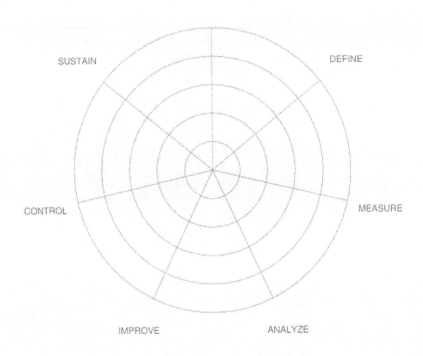

BEGINNING OF THE SELF-ASSESSMENT:

CRITERION #1: RECOGNIZE

INTENT: Be aware of the need for change. Recognize that there is an unfavorable variation, problem or symptom.

In my belief, the answer to this question is clearly defined:

5 Strongly Agree

4 Agree

3 Neutral

2 Disagree

1 Strongly Disagree

1. What situation(s) led to this New Product and Process Development Self Assessment?
<--- Score

2. Is it needed?
<--- Score

3. Which issues are too important to ignore?
<--- Score

4. Are there any specific expectations or concerns about the New Product and Process Development team, New Product and Process Development itself?
<--- Score

5. How are you going to measure success?
<--- Score

6. Who are your key stakeholders who need to sign off?
<--- Score

7. What New Product and Process Development coordination do you need?
<--- Score

8. Looking at each person individually – does every one have the qualities which are needed to work in this group?
<--- Score

9. Are you dealing with any of the same issues today as yesterday? What can you do about this?
<--- Score

10. Where is training needed?
<--- Score

11. Is the quality assurance team identified?
<--- Score

12. What problems are you facing and how do you consider New Product and Process Development will circumvent those obstacles?
<--- Score

13. Do you need to avoid or amend any New Product and Process Development activities?
<--- Score

14. What do you need to start doing?
<--- Score

15. Who needs to know about New Product and Process Development?
<--- Score

16. Will new equipment/products be required to facilitate New Product and Process Development delivery, for example is new software needed?
<--- Score

17. How do you take a forward-looking perspective in identifying New Product and Process Development research related to market response and models?
<--- Score

18. Which needs are not included or involved?
<--- Score

19. What are the New Product and Process Development resources needed?
<--- Score

20. Do you recognize New Product and Process Development achievements?
<--- Score

21. Who else hopes to benefit from it?
<--- Score

22. Do you know what you need to know about New Product and Process Development?
<--- Score

23. To what extent would your organization benefit from being recognized as a award recipient?
<--- Score

24. Consider your own New Product and Process Development project, what types of organizational problems do you think might be causing or affecting your problem, based on the work done so far?
<--- Score

25. What are the timeframes required to resolve each of the issues/problems?
<--- Score

26. Who should resolve the New Product and Process Development issues?
<--- Score

27. What do employees need in the short term?
<--- Score

28. What creative shifts do you need to take?
<--- Score

29. Who needs budgets?
<--- Score

30. What resources or support might you need?
<--- Score

31. What else needs to be measured?
<--- Score

32. Does your organization need more New Product and Process Development education?
<--- Score

33. What should be considered when identifying available resources, constraints, and deadlines?
<--- Score

34. Are problem definition and motivation clearly presented?
<--- Score

35. Will a response program recognize when a crisis occurs and provide some level of response?
<--- Score

36. Have you identified your New Product and Process Development key performance indicators?
<--- Score

37. What activities does the governance board need to consider?
<--- Score

38. What are the stakeholder objectives to be achieved with New Product and Process Development?
<--- Score

39. For your New Product and Process Development project, identify and describe the business environment, is there more than one layer to the business environment?
<--- Score

40. What are the expected benefits of New Product and Process Development to the stakeholder?
<--- Score

41. What is the smallest subset of the problem you can usefully solve?
<--- Score

42. How much are sponsors, customers, partners, stakeholders involved in New Product and Process Development? In other words, what are the risks, if New Product and Process Development does not deliver successfully?
<--- Score

43. What is the problem and/or vulnerability?
<--- Score

44. What vendors make products that address the New Product and Process Development needs?
<--- Score

45. How are training requirements identified?
<--- Score

46. Would you recognize a threat from the inside?
<--- Score

47. When a New Product and Process Development manager recognizes a problem, what options are available?
<--- Score

48. How do you recognize an New Product and Process Development objection?
<--- Score

49. Think about the people you identified for your New Product and Process Development project and the project responsibilities you would assign to them, what kind of training do you think they would need to perform these responsibilities effectively?
<--- Score

50. How many trainings, in total, are needed?
<--- Score

51. Will it solve real problems?
<--- Score

52. Is it clear when you think of the day ahead of you what activities and tasks you need to complete?
<--- Score

53. Do you have/need 24-hour access to key personnel?
<--- Score

54. Does New Product and Process Development create potential expectations in other areas that need to be recognized and considered?
<--- Score

55. Who needs to know?
<--- Score

56. What tools and technologies are needed for a custom New Product and Process Development project?
<--- Score

57. What does New Product and Process Development success mean to the stakeholders?
<--- Score

58. How can auditing be a preventative security measure?
<--- Score

59. What prevents you from making the changes you know will make you a more effective New Product and Process Development leader?
<--- Score

60. Are there regulatory / compliance issues?
<--- Score

61. Where do you need to exercise leadership?
<--- Score

62. Who defines the rules in relation to any given issue?
<--- Score

63. How do you identify subcontractor relationships?
<--- Score

64. Are losses recognized in a timely manner?
<--- Score

65. What training and capacity building actions are needed to implement proposed reforms?
<--- Score

66. Can management personnel recognize the monetary benefit of New Product and Process

Development?

<--- Score

67. What needs to stay?

<--- Score

68. Who needs what information?

<--- Score

69. What New Product and Process Development capabilities do you need?

<--- Score

70. What New Product and Process Development events should you attend?

<--- Score

71. How do you assess your New Product and Process Development workforce capability and capacity needs, including skills, competencies, and staffing levels?

<--- Score

72. Do you need different information or graphics?

<--- Score

73. What is the recognized need?

<--- Score

74. Are controls defined to recognize and contain problems?

<--- Score

75. What are the clients issues and concerns?

<--- Score

76. Did you miss any major New Product and Process Development issues?
<--- Score

77. What needs to be done?
<--- Score

78. What are the minority interests and what amount of minority interests can be recognized?
<--- Score

79. What New Product and Process Development problem should be solved?
<--- Score

80. What is the extent or complexity of the New Product and Process Development problem?
<--- Score

81. How are the New Product and Process Development's objectives aligned to the group's overall stakeholder strategy?
<--- Score

82. To what extent does each concerned units management team recognize New Product and Process Development as an effective investment?
<--- Score

83. How does it fit into your organizational needs and tasks?
<--- Score

84. Are employees recognized for desired behaviors?
<--- Score

85. What information do users need?
<--- Score

86. Are there New Product and Process Development problems defined?
<--- Score

87. What is the New Product and Process Development problem definition? What do you need to resolve?
<--- Score

88. Does the problem have ethical dimensions?
<--- Score

89. What would happen if New Product and Process Development weren't done?
<--- Score

90. How do you identify the kinds of information that you will need?
<--- Score

91. What extra resources will you need?
<--- Score

92. Are there recognized New Product and Process Development problems?
<--- Score

93. What is the problem or issue?
<--- Score

94. As a sponsor, customer or management, how important is it to meet goals, objectives?
<--- Score

95. How do you recognize an objection?
<--- Score

96. Will New Product and Process Development deliverables need to be tested and, if so, by whom?
<--- Score

97. What are your needs in relation to New Product and Process Development skills, labor, equipment, and markets?
<--- Score

98. Why is this needed?
<--- Score

99. Are your goals realistic? Do you need to redefine your problem? Perhaps the problem has changed or maybe you have reached your goal and need to set a new one?
<--- Score

100. Whom do you really need or want to serve?
<--- Score

101. Why the need?
<--- Score

102. Are there any revenue recognition issues?
<--- Score

Add up total points for this section:
_ _ _ _ _ = Total points for this section

Divided by: _ _ _ _ _ _ (number of statements answered) = _ _ _ _ _ _

Average score for this section

Transfer your score to the New Product
and Process Development Index at the
beginning of the Self-Assessment.

CRITERION #2: DEFINE:

INTENT: Formulate the stakeholder problem. Define the problem, needs and objectives.

In my belief, the answer to this question is clearly defined:

5 Strongly Agree

4 Agree

3 Neutral

2 Disagree

1 Strongly Disagree

1. What is the definition of New Product and Process Development excellence?
<--- Score

2. How do you build the right business case?
<--- Score

3. How would you define the culture at your organization, how susceptible is it to New Product

and Process Development changes?
<--- Score

4. How is the team tracking and documenting its work?
<--- Score

5. What are the boundaries of the scope? What is in bounds and what is not? What is the start point? What is the stop point?
<--- Score

6. What was the context?
<--- Score

7. Are there any constraints known that bear on the ability to perform New Product and Process Development work? How is the team addressing them?
<--- Score

8. What are the record-keeping requirements of New Product and Process Development activities?
<--- Score

9. Scope of sensitive information?
<--- Score

10. What happens if New Product and Process Development's scope changes?
<--- Score

11. Is the team adequately staffed with the desired cross-functionality? If not, what additional resources are available to the team?
<--- Score

12. Are required metrics defined, what are they?
<--- Score

13. What key stakeholder process output measure(s) does New Product and Process Development leverage and how?
<--- Score

14. When are meeting minutes sent out? Who is on the distribution list?
<--- Score

15. Are roles and responsibilities formally defined?
<--- Score

16. Who approved the New Product and Process Development scope?
<--- Score

17. Are accountability and ownership for New Product and Process Development clearly defined?
<--- Score

18. How did the New Product and Process Development manager receive input to the development of a New Product and Process Development improvement plan and the estimated completion dates/times of each activity?
<--- Score

19. What is out of scope?
<--- Score

20. What are the New Product and Process Development use cases?

<--- Score

21. Are different versions of process maps needed to account for the different types of inputs?
<--- Score

22. What New Product and Process Development services do you require?
<--- Score

23. What are the New Product and Process Development tasks and definitions?
<--- Score

24. What are (control) requirements for New Product and Process Development Information?
<--- Score

25. What baselines are required to be defined and managed?
<--- Score

26. Is the New Product and Process Development scope complete and appropriately sized?
<--- Score

27. How do you gather the stories?
<--- Score

28. When is/was the New Product and Process Development start date?
<--- Score

29. What is the context?
<--- Score

30. Is the scope of New Product and Process Development defined?
<--- Score

31. What is the scope of New Product and Process Development?
<--- Score

32. Are resources adequate for the scope?
<--- Score

33. Why are you doing New Product and Process Development and what is the scope?
<--- Score

34. Do you have organizational privacy requirements?
<--- Score

35. How was the 'as is' process map developed, reviewed, verified and validated?
<--- Score

36. What constraints exist that might impact the team?
<--- Score

37. What are the compelling stakeholder reasons for embarking on New Product and Process Development?
<--- Score

38. What are the dynamics of the communication plan?
<--- Score

39. Have specific policy objectives been defined?

<--- Score

40. What system do you use for gathering New Product and Process Development information?
<--- Score

41. What is the scope of the New Product and Process Development effort?
<--- Score

42. What is the scope?
<--- Score

43. What are the core elements of the New Product and Process Development business case?
<--- Score

44. What are the tasks and definitions?
<--- Score

45. How are consistent New Product and Process Development definitions important?
<--- Score

46. What are the rough order estimates on cost savings/opportunities that New Product and Process Development brings?
<--- Score

47. When is the estimated completion date?
<--- Score

48. Is there regularly 100% attendance at the team meetings? If not, have appointed substitutes attended to preserve cross-functionality and full representation?

<--- Score

49. What sources do you use to gather information for a New Product and Process Development study?
<--- Score

50. What defines best in class?
<--- Score

51. Has a project plan, Gantt chart, or similar been developed/completed?
<--- Score

52. What are the Roles and Responsibilities for each team member and its leadership? Where is this documented?
<--- Score

53. Has your scope been defined?
<--- Score

54. How do you gather New Product and Process Development requirements?
<--- Score

55. What information do you gather?
<--- Score

56. Are there different segments of customers?
<--- Score

57. Is New Product and Process Development required?
<--- Score

58. Who defines (or who defined) the rules and roles?

<--- Score

59. Has a high-level 'as is' process map been completed, verified and validated?
<--- Score

60. What knowledge or experience is required?
<--- Score

61. Are the New Product and Process Development requirements testable?
<--- Score

62. Does the team have regular meetings?
<--- Score

63. Is there a critical path to deliver New Product and Process Development results?
<--- Score

64. What is in scope?
<--- Score

65. Will a New Product and Process Development production readiness review be required?
<--- Score

66. How and when will the baselines be defined?
<--- Score

67. What scope do you want your strategy to cover?
<--- Score

68. The political context: who holds power?
<--- Score

69. How do you gather requirements?
<--- Score

70. Has everyone on the team, including the team leaders, been properly trained?
<--- Score

71. Is the New Product and Process Development scope manageable?
<--- Score

72. Is there a completed SIPOC representation, describing the Suppliers, Inputs, Process, Outputs, and Customers?
<--- Score

73. Is there a New Product and Process Development management charter, including stakeholder case, problem and goal statements, scope, milestones, roles and responsibilities, communication plan?
<--- Score

74. How do you manage changes in New Product and Process Development requirements?
<--- Score

75. Does the scope remain the same?
<--- Score

76. Is New Product and Process Development currently on schedule according to the plan?
<--- Score

77. Is special New Product and Process Development user knowledge required?

<--- Score

78. What intelligence can you gather?
<--- Score

79. What specifically is the problem? Where does it occur? When does it occur? What is its extent?
<--- Score

80. Do you have a New Product and Process Development success story or case study ready to tell and share?
<--- Score

81. Has a team charter been developed and communicated?
<--- Score

82. What critical content must be communicated – who, what, when, where, and how?
<--- Score

83. How do you think the partners involved in New Product and Process Development would have defined success?
<--- Score

84. How can the value of New Product and Process Development be defined?
<--- Score

85. Where can you gather more information?
<--- Score

86. What is the scope of the New Product and Process Development work?

<--- Score

87. Is there any additional New Product and Process Development definition of success?
<--- Score

88. How do you manage scope?
<--- Score

89. Is New Product and Process Development linked to key stakeholder goals and objectives?
<--- Score

90. What is out-of-scope initially?
<--- Score

91. Is the improvement team aware of the different versions of a process: what they think it is vs. what it actually is vs. what it should be vs. what it could be?
<--- Score

92. Have the customer needs been translated into specific, measurable requirements? How?
<--- Score

93. Are approval levels defined for contracts and supplements to contracts?
<--- Score

94. Are the New Product and Process Development requirements complete?
<--- Score

95. Has a New Product and Process Development requirement not been met?
<--- Score

96. Is the current 'as is' process being followed? If not, what are the discrepancies?
<--- Score

97. What gets examined?
<--- Score

98. What is a worst-case scenario for losses?
<--- Score

99. Has anyone else (internal or external to the group) attempted to solve this problem or a similar one before? If so, what knowledge can be leveraged from these previous efforts?
<--- Score

100. How have you defined all New Product and Process Development requirements first?
<--- Score

101. What is in the scope and what is not in scope?
<--- Score

102. How do you hand over New Product and Process Development context?
<--- Score

103. How do you keep key subject matter experts in the loop?
<--- Score

104. Have all of the relationships been defined properly?
<--- Score

105. Who are the New Product and Process Development improvement team members, including Management Leads and Coaches?
<--- Score

106. Is scope creep really all bad news?
<--- Score

107. Has the direction changed at all during the course of New Product and Process Development? If so, when did it change and why?
<--- Score

108. What would be the goal or target for a New Product and Process Development's improvement team?
<--- Score

109. How often are the team meetings?
<--- Score

110. Is there a completed, verified, and validated high-level 'as is' (not 'should be' or 'could be') stakeholder process map?
<--- Score

111. What is the definition of success?
<--- Score

112. What is the worst case scenario?
<--- Score

113. Are audit criteria, scope, frequency and methods defined?
<--- Score

114. Who is gathering information?
<--- Score

115. How does the New Product and Process
Development manager ensure against scope creep?
<--- Score

116. Who is gathering New Product and Process
Development information?
<--- Score

**117. Have all basic functions of New Product and
Process Development been defined?**
<--- Score

118. Are all requirements met?
<--- Score

119. What New Product and Process Development
requirements should be gathered?
<--- Score

120. If substitutes have been appointed, have
they been briefed on the New Product and
Process Development goals and received regular
communications as to the progress to date?
<--- Score

121. How will the New Product and Process
Development team and the group measure complete
success of New Product and Process Development?
<--- Score

122. In what way can you redefine the criteria of
choice clients have in your category in your favor?
<--- Score

123. Is it clearly defined in and to your organization what you do?

<--- Score

124. How do you manage unclear New Product and Process Development requirements?

<--- Score

125. How will variation in the actual durations of each activity be dealt with to ensure that the expected New Product and Process Development results are met?

<--- Score

126. Do the problem and goal statements meet the SMART criteria (specific, measurable, attainable, relevant, and time-bound)?

<--- Score

127. Is there a clear New Product and Process Development case definition?

<--- Score

128. Has the improvement team collected the 'voice of the customer' (obtained feedback – qualitative and quantitative)?

<--- Score

129. Has the New Product and Process Development work been fairly and/or equitably divided and delegated among team members who are qualified and capable to perform the work? Has everyone contributed?

<--- Score

130. Is data collected and displayed to better

understand customer(s) critical needs and
requirements.
<--- Score

131. What sort of initial information to gather?
<--- Score

132. What customer feedback methods were used to
solicit their input?
<--- Score

133. What are the requirements for audit information?
<--- Score

**134. How do you catch New Product and Process
Development definition inconsistencies?**
<--- Score

135. Has/have the customer(s) been identified?
<--- Score

Add up total points for this section:
_ _ _ _ _ = Total points for this section

Divided by: _ _ _ _ _ _ (number of
statements answered) = _ _ _ _ _ _
Average score for this section

Transfer your score to the New Product
and Process Development Index at the
beginning of the Self-Assessment.

CRITERION #3: MEASURE:

INTENT: Gather the correct data. Measure the current performance and evolution of the situation.

In my belief, the answer to this question is clearly defined:

5 Strongly Agree

4 Agree

3 Neutral

2 Disagree

1 Strongly Disagree

1. What causes innovation to fail or succeed in your organization?
<--- Score

2. Who is involved in verifying compliance?
<--- Score

3. Do the benefits outweigh the costs?
<--- Score

4. Have you made assumptions about the shape of the future, particularly its impact on your customers and competitors?
<--- Score

5. Does the New Product and Process Development task fit the client's priorities?
<--- Score

6. Where can you go to verify the info?
<--- Score

7. Was a business case (cost/benefit) developed?
<--- Score

8. Among the New Product and Process Development product and service cost to be estimated, which is considered hardest to estimate?
<--- Score

9. What evidence is there and what is measured?
<--- Score

10. How do you measure variability?
<--- Score

11. How can you measure the performance?
<--- Score

12. How will effects be measured?
<--- Score

13. How can a New Product and Process Development test verify your ideas or assumptions?
<--- Score

14. What is the root cause(s) of the problem?
<--- Score

15. How do you aggregate measures across priorities?
<--- Score

16. How will success or failure be measured?
<--- Score

17. What would be a real cause for concern?
<--- Score

18. Have you included everything in your New Product and Process Development cost models?
<--- Score

19. What is the total fixed cost?
<--- Score

20. Are you able to realize any cost savings?
<--- Score

21. How will costs be allocated?
<--- Score

22. Does a New Product and Process Development quantification method exist?
<--- Score

23. What are you verifying?
<--- Score

24. Why a New Product and Process Development focus?
<--- Score

25. What are your key New Product and Process Development organizational performance measures, including key short and longer-term financial measures?
<--- Score

26. How do your measurements capture actionable New Product and Process Development information for use in exceeding your customers expectations and securing your customers engagement?
<--- Score

27. What does a Test Case verify?
<--- Score

28. How is progress measured?
<--- Score

29. What are the estimated costs of proposed changes?
<--- Score

30. When a disaster occurs, who gets priority?
<--- Score

31. What harm might be caused?
<--- Score

32. Will New Product and Process Development have an impact on current business continuity, disaster recovery processes and/or infrastructure?
<--- Score

33. What are the costs of delaying New Product and Process Development action?

<--- Score

34. How are costs allocated?
<--- Score

35. How is performance measured?
<--- Score

36. Are you taking your company in the direction of better and revenue or cheaper and cost?
<--- Score

37. What causes extra work or rework?
<--- Score

38. What is your New Product and Process Development quality cost segregation study?
<--- Score

39. Have design-to-cost goals been established?
<--- Score

40. How to cause the change?
<--- Score

41. What disadvantage does this cause for the user?
<--- Score

42. Why do you expend time and effort to implement measurement, for whom?
<--- Score

43. How do you verify New Product and Process Development completeness and accuracy?
<--- Score

44. What is the cost of rework?
<--- Score

45. What relevant entities could be measured?
<--- Score

46. What could cause delays in the schedule?
<--- Score

47. What methods are feasible and acceptable to estimate the impact of reforms?
<--- Score

48. How do you verify your resources?
<--- Score

49. Did you tackle the cause or the symptom?
<--- Score

50. How do you verify if New Product and Process Development is built right?
<--- Score

51. Is the solution cost-effective?
<--- Score

52. How will you measure success?
<--- Score

53. What causes investor action?
<--- Score

54. Do you verify that corrective actions were taken?
<--- Score

55. How are measurements made?

<--- Score

56. How do you verify and develop ideas and innovations?
<--- Score

57. How sensitive must the New Product and Process Development strategy be to cost?
<--- Score

58. What does losing customers cost your organization?
<--- Score

59. Who should receive measurement reports?
<--- Score

60. What are allowable costs?
<--- Score

61. Is it possible to estimate the impact of unanticipated complexity such as wrong or failed assumptions, feedback, etcetera on proposed reforms?
<--- Score

62. When should you bother with diagrams?
<--- Score

63. How do you verify the authenticity of the data and information used?
<--- Score

64. How will measures be used to manage and adapt?
<--- Score

65. How do you prevent mis-estimating cost?
<--- Score

66. What are your primary costs, revenues, assets?
<--- Score

67. How much does it cost?
<--- Score

68. How will you measure your New Product and
Process Development effectiveness?
<--- Score

69. What is measured? Why?
<--- Score

70. What is the cause of any New Product and Process
Development gaps?
<--- Score

71. How are you verifying it?
<--- Score

72. Are there competing New Product and Process
Development priorities?
<--- Score

73. How can you measure New Product and Process
Development in a systematic way?
<--- Score

**74. Is the cost worth the New Product and Process
Development effort ?**
<--- Score

75. What do people want to verify?

<--- Score

76. How do you measure lifecycle phases?
<--- Score

77. How can you reduce costs?
<--- Score

78. How frequently do you track New Product and Process Development measures?
<--- Score

79. Are New Product and Process Development vulnerabilities categorized and prioritized?
<--- Score

80. Does management have the right priorities among projects?
<--- Score

81. Has a cost center been established?
<--- Score

82. How is the value delivered by New Product and Process Development being measured?
<--- Score

83. Which measures and indicators matter?
<--- Score

84. Do you have a flow diagram of what happens?
<--- Score

85. Is there an opportunity to verify requirements?
<--- Score

86. What is your decision requirements diagram?
<--- Score

87. Are actual costs in line with budgeted costs?
<--- Score

88. Who pays the cost?
<--- Score

89. Are you aware of what could cause a problem?
<--- Score

90. Are supply costs steady or fluctuating?
<--- Score

91. How do you verify the New Product and Process
Development requirements quality?
<--- Score

92. What tests verify requirements?
<--- Score

93. What are your operating costs?
<--- Score

94. At what cost?
<--- Score

**95. Do you effectively measure and reward
individual and team performance?**
<--- Score

96. What measurements are possible, practicable and
meaningful?
<--- Score

97. What causes mismanagement?
<--- Score

98. What are the New Product and Process Development key cost drivers?
<--- Score

99. What is the total cost related to deploying New Product and Process Development, including any consulting or professional services?
<--- Score

100. What does your operating model cost?
<--- Score

101. What are the costs of reform?
<--- Score

102. How do you measure efficient delivery of New Product and Process Development services?
<--- Score

103. What are your customers expectations and measures?
<--- Score

104. What are the current costs of the New Product and Process Development process?
<--- Score

105. What is the New Product and Process Development business impact?
<--- Score

106. How do you control the overall costs of your work processes?

<--- Score

107. What is an unallowable cost?
<--- Score

108. What could cause you to change course?
<--- Score

109. What are the costs?
<--- Score

110. How frequently do you verify your New Product and Process Development strategy?
<--- Score

111. How do you measure success?
<--- Score

112. What happens if cost savings do not materialize?
<--- Score

113. What are the uncertainties surrounding estimates of impact?
<--- Score

114. How do you verify and validate the New Product and Process Development data?
<--- Score

115. When are costs are incurred?
<--- Score

116. What are the operational costs after New Product and Process Development deployment?
<--- Score

117. Do you have any cost New Product and Process Development limitation requirements?
<--- Score

118. Are there measurements based on task performance?
<--- Score

119. Do you have an issue in getting priority?
<--- Score

120. Which costs should be taken into account?
<--- Score

121. How can you manage cost down?
<--- Score

122. Why do the measurements/indicators matter?
<--- Score

123. What would it cost to replace your technology?
<--- Score

124. What do you measure and why?
<--- Score

125. What are the strategic priorities for this year?
<--- Score

126. Are there any easy-to-implement alternatives to New Product and Process Development? Sometimes other solutions are available that do not require the cost implications of a full-blown project?
<--- Score

127. Are the units of measure consistent?

<--- Score

128. What can be used to verify compliance?

<--- Score

129. How do you verify performance?

<--- Score

130. The approach of traditional New Product and Process Development works for detail complexity but is focused on a systematic approach rather than an understanding of the nature of systems themselves, what approach will permit your organization to deal with the kind of unpredictable emergent behaviors that dynamic complexity can introduce?

<--- Score

131. What are the types and number of measures to use?

<--- Score

132. What are the New Product and Process Development investment costs?

<--- Score

133. Are the New Product and Process Development benefits worth its costs?

<--- Score

134. What details are required of the New Product and Process Development cost structure?

<--- Score

Add up total points for this section:
_ _ _ _ _ = Total points for this section

Divided by: _ _ _ _ _ _ (number of
statements answered) = _ _ _ _ _ _
Average score for this section

Transfer your score to the New Product
and Process Development Index at the
beginning of the Self-Assessment.

CRITERION #4: ANALYZE:

INTENT: Analyze causes, assumptions and hypotheses.

In my belief, the answer to this question is clearly defined:

5 Strongly Agree

4 Agree

3 Neutral

2 Disagree

1 Strongly Disagree

1. What qualifies as competition?
<--- Score

2. Do staff qualifications match your project?
<--- Score

3. What are your current levels and trends in key measures or indicators of New Product and Process Development product and process performance that are important to and directly serve your customers?

How do these results compare with the performance of your competitors and other organizations with similar offerings?
<--- Score

4. Has an output goal been set?
<--- Score

5. What are the disruptive New Product and Process Development technologies that enable your organization to radically change your business processes?
<--- Score

6. Was a cause-and-effect diagram used to explore the different types of causes (or sources of variation)?
<--- Score

7. What are evaluation criteria for the output?
<--- Score

8. Is there an established change management process?
<--- Score

9. What is the complexity of the output produced?
<--- Score

10. How is the way you as the leader think and process information affecting your organizational culture?
<--- Score

11. What are the New Product and Process Development business drivers?
<--- Score

12. Is data and process analysis, root cause analysis and quantifying the gap/opportunity in place?
<--- Score

13. Do you understand your management processes today?
<--- Score

14. Were there any improvement opportunities identified from the process analysis?
<--- Score

15. How do you implement and manage your work processes to ensure that they meet design requirements?
<--- Score

16. What is the oversight process?
<--- Score

17. How do your work systems and key work processes relate to and capitalize on your core competencies?
<--- Score

18. What controls do you have in place to protect data?
<--- Score

19. What are your key performance measures or indicators and in-process measures for the control and improvement of your New Product and Process Development processes?
<--- Score

20. Have any additional benefits been identified that

will result from closing all or most of the gaps?
<--- Score

21. What successful thing are you doing today that may be blinding you to new growth opportunities?
<--- Score

22. What quality tools were used to get through the analyze phase?
<--- Score

23. How difficult is it to qualify what New Product and Process Development ROI is?
<--- Score

24. What resources go in to get the desired output?
<--- Score

25. What kind of crime could a potential new hire have committed that would not only not disqualify him/her from being hired by your organization, but would actually indicate that he/she might be a particularly good fit?
<--- Score

26. What are your best practices for minimizing New Product and Process Development project risk, while demonstrating incremental value and quick wins throughout the New Product and Process Development project lifecycle?
<--- Score

27. What are the processes for audit reporting and management?
<--- Score

28. Have the problem and goal statements been updated to reflect the additional knowledge gained from the analyze phase?

<--- Score

29. Do you have the authority to produce the output?

<--- Score

30. How many input/output points does it require?

<--- Score

31. Are all staff in core New Product and Process Development subjects Highly Qualified?

<--- Score

32. Who is involved in the management review process?

<--- Score

33. Did any additional data need to be collected?

<--- Score

34. What training and qualifications will you need?

<--- Score

35. Record-keeping requirements flow from the records needed as inputs, outputs, controls and for transformation of a New Product and Process Development process, are the records needed as inputs to the New Product and Process Development process available?

<--- Score

36. How is the data gathered?

<--- Score

37. Are you missing New Product and Process Development opportunities?

<--- Score

38. A compounding model resolution with available relevant data can often provide insight towards a solution methodology; which New Product and Process Development models, tools and techniques are necessary?

<--- Score

39. Is there a strict change management process?

<--- Score

40. Are all team members qualified for all tasks?

<--- Score

41. How is New Product and Process Development data gathered?

<--- Score

42. Do your leaders quickly bounce back from setbacks?

<--- Score

43. How is the New Product and Process Development Value Stream Mapping managed?

<--- Score

44. Do you, as a leader, bounce back quickly from setbacks?

<--- Score

45. Is the New Product and Process Development process severely broken such that a re-design is

necessary?

<--- Score

46. What tools were used to generate the list of possible causes?

<--- Score

47. An organizationally feasible system request is one that considers the mission, goals and objectives of the organization, key questions are: is the New Product and Process Development solution request practical and will it solve a problem or take advantage of an opportunity to achieve company goals?

<--- Score

48. What did the team gain from developing a sub-process map?

<--- Score

49. Are your outputs consistent?

<--- Score

50. Think about the functions involved in your New Product and Process Development project, what processes flow from these functions?

<--- Score

51. What other jobs or tasks affect the performance of the steps in the New Product and Process Development process?

<--- Score

52. How do you use New Product and Process Development data and information to support organizational decision making and innovation?

<--- Score

53. Which New Product and Process Development data should be retained?
<--- Score

54. What are the best opportunities for value improvement?
<--- Score

55. Have you defined which data is gathered how?
<--- Score

56. How do you identify specific New Product and Process Development investment opportunities and emerging trends?
<--- Score

57. How are outputs preserved and protected?
<--- Score

58. Is the suppliers process defined and controlled?
<--- Score

59. What systems/processes must you excel at?
<--- Score

60. How will the New Product and Process Development data be captured?
<--- Score

61. What are the revised rough estimates of the financial savings/opportunity for New Product and Process Development improvements?
<--- Score

62. How can risk management be tied procedurally to process elements?
<--- Score

63. What New Product and Process Development data will be collected?
<--- Score

64. Is the performance gap determined?
<--- Score

65. What New Product and Process Development metrics are outputs of the process?
<--- Score

66. What are your New Product and Process Development processes?
<--- Score

67. What will drive New Product and Process Development change?
<--- Score

68. How do mission and objectives affect the New Product and Process Development processes of your organization?
<--- Score

69. What output to create?
<--- Score

70. Should you invest in industry-recognized qualifications?
<--- Score

71. What information qualified as important?

<--- Score

72. Do several people in different organizational units assist with the New Product and Process Development process?
<--- Score

73. What qualifications and skills do you need?
<--- Score

74. Is pre-qualification of suppliers carried out?
<--- Score

75. How is data used for program management and improvement?
<--- Score

76. How do you measure the operational performance of your key work systems and processes, including productivity, cycle time, and other appropriate measures of process effectiveness, efficiency, and innovation?
<--- Score

77. What conclusions were drawn from the team's data collection and analysis? How did the team reach these conclusions?
<--- Score

78. What qualifications are necessary?
<--- Score

79. What New Product and Process Development data should be managed?
<--- Score

80. Who will gather what data?
<--- Score

81. Are gaps between current performance and the goal performance identified?
<--- Score

82. What is the New Product and Process Development Driver?
<--- Score

83. Were any designed experiments used to generate additional insight into the data analysis?
<--- Score

84. Identify an operational issue in your organization, for example, could a particular task be done more quickly or more efficiently by New Product and Process Development?
<--- Score

85. Can you add value to the current New Product and Process Development decision-making process (largely qualitative) by incorporating uncertainty modeling (more quantitative)?
<--- Score

86. What is the output?
<--- Score

87. Is the gap/opportunity displayed and communicated in financial terms?
<--- Score

88. How much data can be collected in the given timeframe?

<--- Score

89. Is the required New Product and Process Development data gathered?
<--- Score

90. Where can you get qualified talent today?
<--- Score

91. Where is the data coming from to measure compliance?
<--- Score

92. What are your current levels and trends in key New Product and Process Development measures or indicators of product and process performance that are important to and directly serve your customers?
<--- Score

93. How was the detailed process map generated, verified, and validated?
<--- Score

94. What methods do you use to gather New Product and Process Development data?
<--- Score

95. How do you promote understanding that opportunity for improvement is not criticism of the status quo, or the people who created the status quo?
<--- Score

96. What New Product and Process Development data should be collected?

<--- Score

97. What were the crucial 'moments of truth' on the process map?
<--- Score

98. How will the change process be managed?
<--- Score

99. What is the Value Stream Mapping?
<--- Score

100. What is your organizations system for selecting qualified vendors?
<--- Score

101. What do you need to qualify?
<--- Score

102. Has data output been validated?
<--- Score

103. How will the data be checked for quality?
<--- Score

104. Do quality systems drive continuous improvement?
<--- Score

105. Where is New Product and Process Development data gathered?
<--- Score

106. How will corresponding data be collected?
<--- Score

107. Do your contracts/agreements contain data security obligations?
<--- Score

108. What were the financial benefits resulting from any 'ground fruit or low-hanging fruit' (quick fixes)?
<--- Score

109. What data is gathered?
<--- Score

110. How does the organization define, manage, and improve its New Product and Process Development processes?
<--- Score

111. Do your employees have the opportunity to do what they do best everyday?
<--- Score

112. What qualifications are needed?
<--- Score

113. What internal processes need improvement?
<--- Score

114. What is the cost of poor quality as supported by the team's analysis?
<--- Score

115. Did any value-added analysis or 'lean thinking' take place to identify some of the gaps shown on the 'as is' process map?
<--- Score

116. What are the New Product and Process

Development design outputs?

<--- Score

117. Who owns what data?

<--- Score

118. How do you define collaboration and team output?

<--- Score

119. What process improvements will be needed?

<--- Score

120. What are your outputs?

<--- Score

121. What, related to, New Product and Process Development processes does your organization outsource?

<--- Score

122. Is the final output clearly identified?

<--- Score

123. Were Pareto charts (or similar) used to portray the 'heavy hitters' (or key sources of variation)?

<--- Score

124. Think about some of the processes you undertake within your organization, which do you own?

<--- Score

125. Who gets your output?

<--- Score

126. Who qualifies to gain access to data?
<--- Score

127. When should a process be art not science?
<--- Score

128. Are New Product and Process Development changes recognized early enough to be approved through the regular process?
<--- Score

129. What types of data do your New Product and Process Development indicators require?
<--- Score

130. What qualifications do New Product and Process Development leaders need?
<--- Score

131. What are the personnel training and qualifications required?
<--- Score

132. What are the necessary qualifications?
<--- Score

133. Was a detailed process map created to amplify critical steps of the 'as is' stakeholder process?
<--- Score

134. How has the New Product and Process Development data been gathered?
<--- Score

135. What does the data say about the performance of the stakeholder process?

<--- Score

136. What tools were used to narrow the list of possible causes?
<--- Score

Add up total points for this section:
_____ = Total points for this section

Divided by: _____ (number of statements answered) = _____
Average score for this section

Transfer your score to the New Product and Process Development Index at the beginning of the Self-Assessment.

CRITERION #5: IMPROVE:

INTENT: Develop a practical solution. Innovate, establish and test the solution and to measure the results.

In my belief, the answer to this question is clearly defined:

5 Strongly Agree

4 Agree

3 Neutral

2 Disagree

1 Strongly Disagree

1. Which New Product and Process Development solution is appropriate?
<--- Score

2. What tools do you use once you have decided on a New Product and Process Development strategy and more importantly how do you choose?
<--- Score

3. What to do with the results or outcomes of measurements?
<--- Score

4. Have you identified breakpoints and/or risk tolerances that will trigger broad consideration of a potential need for intervention or modification of strategy?
<--- Score

5. How do you decide how much to remunerate an employee?
<--- Score

6. Risk events: what are the things that could go wrong?
<--- Score

7. Is risk periodically assessed?
<--- Score

8. How do the New Product and Process Development results compare with the performance of your competitors and other organizations with similar offerings?
<--- Score

9. How do you go about comparing New Product and Process Development approaches/solutions?
<--- Score

10. What tools were used to tap into the creativity and encourage 'outside the box' thinking?
<--- Score

11. Can you integrate quality management and risk

management?

<--- Score

12. What are the concrete New Product and Process Development results?

<--- Score

13. How can you improve New Product and Process Development?

<--- Score

14. Who are the key stakeholders for the New Product and Process Development evaluation?

<--- Score

15. Can you identify any significant risks or exposures to New Product and Process Development third- parties (vendors, service providers, alliance partners etc) that concern you?

<--- Score

16. What attendant changes will need to be made to ensure that the solution is successful?

<--- Score

17. How do you measure improved New Product and Process Development service perception, and satisfaction?

<--- Score

18. Which of the recognised risks out of all risks can be most likely transferred?

<--- Score

19. What practices helps your organization to develop its capacity to recognize patterns?

<--- Score

20. How can you improve performance?
<--- Score

21. What communications are necessary to support the implementation of the solution?
<--- Score

22. Do you need to do a usability evaluation?
<--- Score

23. Is there any other New Product and Process Development solution?
<--- Score

24. How do you mitigate New Product and Process Development risk?
<--- Score

25. How can you better manage risk?
<--- Score

26. Have you achieved New Product and Process Development improvements?
<--- Score

27. How significant is the improvement in the eyes of the end user?
<--- Score

28. How are New Product and Process Development risks managed?
<--- Score

29. Do vendor agreements bring new compliance risk

?
<--- Score

30. How do you keep improving New Product and Process Development?
<--- Score

31. Is any New Product and Process Development documentation required?
<--- Score

32. Risk factors: what are the characteristics of New Product and Process Development that make it risky?
<--- Score

33. What were the criteria for evaluating a New Product and Process Development pilot?
<--- Score

34. Where do the New Product and Process Development decisions reside?
<--- Score

35. Are the risks fully understood, reasonable and manageable?
<--- Score

36. What tools were used to evaluate the potential solutions?
<--- Score

37. Is the New Product and Process Development solution sustainable?
<--- Score

38. Who will be using the results of the

measurement activities?
<--- Score

39. Would you develop a New Product and Process Development Communication Strategy?
<--- Score

40. Is the scope clearly documented?
<--- Score

41. Are risk triggers captured?
<--- Score

42. How do you improve your likelihood of success ?
<--- Score

43. Who are the people involved in developing and implementing New Product and Process Development?
<--- Score

44. Is the New Product and Process Development risk managed?
<--- Score

45. How are policy decisions made and where?
<--- Score

46. Who manages New Product and Process Development risk?
<--- Score

47. How do you measure risk?
<--- Score

48. How is continuous improvement applied to risk

management?
<--- Score

49. What is New Product and Process Development's impact on utilizing the best solution(s)?
<--- Score

50. Who should make the New Product and Process Development decisions?
<--- Score

51. Risk Identification: What are the possible risk events your organization faces in relation to New Product and Process Development?
<--- Score

52. Is there a high likelihood that any recommendations will achieve their intended results?
<--- Score

53. What is the magnitude of the improvements?
<--- Score

54. Who are the New Product and Process Development decision makers?
<--- Score

55. Are the most efficient solutions problem-specific?
<--- Score

56. Who will be responsible for making the decisions to include or exclude requested changes once New Product and Process Development is underway?
<--- Score

57. What is the New Product and Process

Development's sustainability risk?
<--- Score

58. How do you measure progress and evaluate training effectiveness?
<--- Score

59. How do you manage and improve your New Product and Process Development work systems to deliver customer value and achieve organizational success and sustainability?
<--- Score

60. What tools were most useful during the improve phase?
<--- Score

61. Are the key business and technology risks being managed?
<--- Score

62. What is New Product and Process Development risk?
<--- Score

63. What is the risk?
<--- Score

64. Who controls key decisions that will be made?
<--- Score

65. How does your organization evaluate strategic New Product and Process Development success?
<--- Score

66. What are the expected New Product and

Process Development results?
<--- Score

67. What assumptions are made about the solution and approach?
<--- Score

68. What is the implementation plan?
<--- Score

69. For estimation problems, how do you develop an estimation statement?
<--- Score

70. Is there a cost/benefit analysis of optimal solution(s)?
<--- Score

71. Is the optimal solution selected based on testing and analysis?
<--- Score

72. What lessons, if any, from a pilot were incorporated into the design of the full-scale solution?
<--- Score

73. How do you improve productivity?
<--- Score

74. To what extent does management recognize New Product and Process Development as a tool to increase the results?
<--- Score

75. How will you know that a change is an improvement?

<--- Score

76. What are the New Product and Process Development security risks?
<--- Score

77. In the past few months, what is the smallest change you have made that has had the biggest positive result? What was it about that small change that produced the large return?
<--- Score

78. Who makes the New Product and Process Development decisions in your organization?
<--- Score

79. Is the solution technically practical?
<--- Score

80. Is the measure of success for New Product and Process Development understandable to a variety of people?
<--- Score

81. Who do you report New Product and Process Development results to?
<--- Score

82. Does a good decision guarantee a good outcome?
<--- Score

83. What resources are required for the improvement efforts?
<--- Score

84. Can the solution be designed and

implemented within an acceptable time period?
<--- Score

85. Who will be responsible for documenting the New Product and Process Development requirements in detail?
<--- Score

86. How scalable is your New Product and Process Development solution?
<--- Score

87. Do you combine technical expertise with business knowledge and New Product and Process Development Key topics include lifecycles, development approaches, requirements and how to make a business case?
<--- Score

88. What does the 'should be' process map/design look like?
<--- Score

89. If you could go back in time five years, what decision would you make differently? What is your best guess as to what decision you're making today you might regret five years from now?
<--- Score

90. Were any criteria developed to assist the team in testing and evaluating potential solutions?
<--- Score

91. What area needs the greatest improvement?
<--- Score

92. What is the team's contingency plan for potential problems occurring in implementation?
<--- Score

93. How will you know that you have improved?
<--- Score

94. What actually has to improve and by how much?
<--- Score

95. What are the affordable New Product and Process Development risks?
<--- Score

96. What should a proof of concept or pilot accomplish?
<--- Score

97. How will you measure the results?
<--- Score

98. What strategies for New Product and Process Development improvement are successful?
<--- Score

99. What needs improvement? Why?
<--- Score

100. What do you want to improve?
<--- Score

101. How can skill-level changes improve New Product and Process Development?
<--- Score

102. Do those selected for the New Product and

Process Development team have a good general understanding of what New Product and Process Development is all about?
<--- Score

103. At what point will vulnerability assessments be performed once New Product and Process Development is put into production (e.g., ongoing Risk Management after implementation)?
<--- Score

104. Was a pilot designed for the proposed solution(s)?
<--- Score

105. How do you improve New Product and Process Development service perception, and satisfaction?
<--- Score

106. How do you deal with New Product and Process Development risk?
<--- Score

107. How will you recognize and celebrate results?
<--- Score

108. How risky is your organization?
<--- Score

109. What were the underlying assumptions on the cost-benefit analysis?
<--- Score

110. What are your current levels and trends in key measures or indicators of workforce and leader development?

<--- Score

111. How do you manage New Product and Process Development risk?
<--- Score

112. Explorations of the frontiers of New Product and Process Development will help you build influence, improve New Product and Process Development, optimize decision making, and sustain change, what is your approach?
<--- Score

113. How does the team improve its work?
<--- Score

114. What error proofing will be done to address some of the discrepancies observed in the 'as is' process?
<--- Score

115. Why improve in the first place?
<--- Score

116. What criteria will you use to assess your New Product and Process Development risks?
<--- Score

117. Are procedures documented for managing New Product and Process Development risks?
<--- Score

118. Do you have the optimal project management team structure?
<--- Score

119. Will the controls trigger any other risks?

<--- Score

120. What current systems have to be understood and/or changed?
<--- Score

121. Who manages supplier risk management in your organization?
<--- Score

122. Are decisions made in a timely manner?
<--- Score

123. What can you do to improve?
<--- Score

124. For decision problems, how do you develop a decision statement?
<--- Score

125. New Product and Process Development risk decisions: whose call Is It?
<--- Score

126. Is supporting New Product and Process Development documentation required?
<--- Score

127. What went well, what should change, what can improve?
<--- Score

128. Was a New Product and Process Development charter developed?
<--- Score

129. What are the implications of the one critical New Product and Process Development decision 10 minutes, 10 months, and 10 years from now?
<--- Score

130. How can the phases of New Product and Process Development development be identified?
<--- Score

131. When you map the key players in your own work and the types/domains of relationships with them, which relationships do you find easy and which challenging, and why?
<--- Score

132. Is there a small-scale pilot for proposed improvement(s)? What conclusions were drawn from the outcomes of a pilot?
<--- Score

133. What improvements have been achieved?
<--- Score

134. How will you know when its improved?
<--- Score

135. Where do you need New Product and Process Development improvement?
<--- Score

136. Who are the New Product and Process Development decision-makers?
<--- Score

Add up total points for this section:
_ _ _ _ _ = Total points for this section

Divided by: _____ (number of
statements answered) = _____
Average score for this section

Transfer your score to the New Product
and Process Development Index at the
beginning of the Self-Assessment.

CRITERION #6: CONTROL:

INTENT: Implement the practical
solution. Maintain the performance and
correct possible complications.

In my belief, the answer to this
question is clearly defined:

5 Strongly Agree

4 Agree

3 Neutral

2 Disagree

1 Strongly Disagree

**1. How can you best use all of your knowledge
repositories to enhance learning and sharing?**
<--- Score

2. Does job training on the documented procedures
need to be part of the process team's education and
training?
<--- Score

3. Act/Adjust: What Do you Need to Do Differently?
<--- Score

4. Is a response plan established and deployed?
<--- Score

5. Are documented procedures clear and easy to follow for the operators?
<--- Score

6. How likely is the current New Product and Process Development plan to come in on schedule or on budget?
<--- Score

7. Implementation Planning: is a pilot needed to test the changes before a full roll out occurs?
<--- Score

8. How will report readings be checked to effectively monitor performance?
<--- Score

9. Do the New Product and Process Development decisions you make today help people and the planet tomorrow?
<--- Score

10. How will new or emerging customer needs/requirements be checked/communicated to orient the process toward meeting the new specifications and continually reducing variation?
<--- Score

11. What are customers monitoring?
<--- Score

12. What is the control/monitoring plan?
<--- Score

13. How do your controls stack up?
<--- Score

14. Do you monitor the effectiveness of your New Product and Process Development activities?
<--- Score

15. Does the New Product and Process Development performance meet the customer's requirements?
<--- Score

16. How widespread is its use?
<--- Score

17. Will existing staff require re-training, for example, to learn new business processes?
<--- Score

18. Is knowledge gained on process shared and institutionalized?
<--- Score

19. Have new or revised work instructions resulted?
<--- Score

20. Has the improved process and its steps been standardized?
<--- Score

21. Will your goals reflect your program budget?
<--- Score

22. What are the critical parameters to watch?
<--- Score

23. How is New Product and Process Development project cost planned, managed, monitored?
<--- Score

24. Where do ideas that reach policy makers and planners as proposals for New Product and Process Development strengthening and reform actually originate?
<--- Score

25. Is reporting being used or needed?
<--- Score

26. Is there a documented and implemented monitoring plan?
<--- Score

27. What is the standard for acceptable New Product and Process Development performance?
<--- Score

28. How do controls support value?
<--- Score

29. What should the next improvement project be that is related to New Product and Process Development?
<--- Score

30. Has the New Product and Process Development value of standards been quantified?
<--- Score

31. Are the New Product and Process Development standards challenging?
<--- Score

32. Is there a New Product and Process Development Communication plan covering who needs to get what information when?
<--- Score

33. How do you plan on providing proper recognition and disclosure of supporting companies?
<--- Score

34. What is your plan to assess your security risks?
<--- Score

35. Who will be in control?
<--- Score

36. Who is going to spread your message?
<--- Score

37. How do you establish and deploy modified action plans if circumstances require a shift in plans and rapid execution of new plans?
<--- Score

38. Can you adapt and adjust to changing New Product and Process Development situations?
<--- Score

39. Does New Product and Process Development appropriately measure and monitor risk?
<--- Score

40. What adjustments to the strategies are

needed?
<--- Score

41. Is there documentation that will support the successful operation of the improvement?
<--- Score

42. How will New Product and Process Development decisions be made and monitored?
<--- Score

43. Is there a recommended audit plan for routine surveillance inspections of New Product and Process Development's gains?
<--- Score

44. What can you control?
<--- Score

45. Are new process steps, standards, and documentation ingrained into normal operations?
<--- Score

46. Can support from partners be adjusted?
<--- Score

47. Against what alternative is success being measured?
<--- Score

48. What are the key elements of your New Product and Process Development performance improvement system, including your evaluation, organizational learning, and innovation processes?
<--- Score

49. What other areas of the group might benefit from the New Product and Process Development team's improvements, knowledge, and learning?
<--- Score

50. How will input, process, and output variables be checked to detect for sub-optimal conditions?
<--- Score

51. How will the day-to-day responsibilities for monitoring and continual improvement be transferred from the improvement team to the process owner?
<--- Score

52. What is the recommended frequency of auditing?
<--- Score

53. Are suggested corrective/restorative actions indicated on the response plan for known causes to problems that might surface?
<--- Score

54. What are you attempting to measure/monitor?
<--- Score

55. What New Product and Process Development standards are applicable?
<--- Score

56. Are pertinent alerts monitored, analyzed and distributed to appropriate personnel?
<--- Score

57. Is the New Product and Process Development test/ monitoring cost justified?

<--- Score

58. Is a response plan in place for when the input, process, or output measures indicate an 'out-of-control' condition?
<--- Score

59. Is there a transfer of ownership and knowledge to process owner and process team tasked with the responsibilities.
<--- Score

60. How do you plan for the cost of succession?
<--- Score

61. How will the process owner verify improvement in present and future sigma levels, process capabilities?
<--- Score

62. What is the best design framework for New Product and Process Development organization now that, in a post industrial-age if the top-down, command and control model is no longer relevant?
<--- Score

63. Are controls in place and consistently applied?
<--- Score

64. What are your results for key measures or indicators of the accomplishment of your New Product and Process Development strategy and action plans, including building and strengthening core competencies?
<--- Score

65. You may have created your quality measures at a

time when you lacked resources, technology wasn't up to the required standard, or low service levels were the industry norm. Have those circumstances changed?
<--- Score

66. How do senior leaders actions reflect a commitment to the organizations New Product and Process Development values?
<--- Score

67. Is there an action plan in case of emergencies?
<--- Score

68. What key inputs and outputs are being measured on an ongoing basis?
<--- Score

69. Is there a standardized process?
<--- Score

70. How might the group capture best practices and lessons learned so as to leverage improvements?
<--- Score

71. What do you measure to verify effectiveness gains?
<--- Score

72. Who controls critical resources?
<--- Score

73. Are operating procedures consistent?
<--- Score

74. Does a troubleshooting guide exist or is it needed?

<--- Score

75. Will any special training be provided for results interpretation?
<--- Score

76. Is there a control plan in place for sustaining improvements (short and long-term)?
<--- Score

77. What quality tools were useful in the control phase?
<--- Score

78. What should you measure to verify efficiency gains?
<--- Score

79. How do you monitor usage and cost?
<--- Score

80. Does the response plan contain a definite closed loop continual improvement scheme (e.g., plan-do-check-act)?
<--- Score

81. How do you spread information?
<--- Score

82. What is your theory of human motivation, and how does your compensation plan fit with that view?
<--- Score

83. How is change control managed?
<--- Score

84. Are the planned controls in place?
<--- Score

85. Who is the New Product and Process Development process owner?
<--- Score

86. What do your reports reflect?
<--- Score

87. Is new knowledge gained imbedded in the response plan?
<--- Score

88. How do you select, collect, align, and integrate New Product and Process Development data and information for tracking daily operations and overall organizational performance, including progress relative to strategic objectives and action plans?
<--- Score

89. Are there documented procedures?
<--- Score

90. How will the process owner and team be able to hold the gains?
<--- Score

91. What other systems, operations, processes, and infrastructures (hiring practices, staffing, training, incentives/rewards, metrics/dashboards/scorecards, etc.) need updates, additions, changes, or deletions in order to facilitate knowledge transfer and improvements?
<--- Score

92. Do you monitor the New Product and Process Development decisions made and fine tune them as they evolve?
<--- Score

Add up total points for this section:
_____ = Total points for this section

Divided by: _____ (number of statements answered) = _____
Average score for this section

Transfer your score to the New Product and Process Development Index at the beginning of the Self-Assessment.

CRITERION #7: SUSTAIN:

INTENT: Retain the benefits.

In my belief, the answer to this question is clearly defined:

5 Strongly Agree

4 Agree

3 Neutral

2 Disagree

1 Strongly Disagree

1. If you were responsible for initiating and implementing major changes in your organization, what steps might you take to ensure acceptance of those changes?
<--- Score

2. What is the estimated value of the project?
<--- Score

3. Is there any reason to believe the opposite of my current belief?

<--- Score

4. If there were zero limitations, what would you do differently?
<--- Score

5. What are internal and external New Product and Process Development relations?
<--- Score

6. Who will provide the final approval of New Product and Process Development deliverables?
<--- Score

7. To whom do you add value?
<--- Score

8. Who are the key stakeholders?
<--- Score

9. Do you think New Product and Process Development accomplishes the goals you expect it to accomplish?
<--- Score

10. In a project to restructure New Product and Process Development outcomes, which stakeholders would you involve?
<--- Score

11. How can you become the company that would put you out of business?
<--- Score

12. If you weren't already in this business, would you enter it today? And if not, what are you going to do

about it?
<--- Score

13. What stupid rule would you most like to kill?
<--- Score

14. What are the usability implications of New Product
and Process Development actions?
<--- Score

15. Who is responsible for errors?
<--- Score

16. What is the recommended frequency of auditing?
<--- Score

17. If no one would ever find out about your
accomplishments, how would you lead differently?
<--- Score

**18. Why will customers want to buy your
organizations products/services?**
<--- Score

19. Is a New Product and Process Development team
work effort in place?
<--- Score

20. Will it be accepted by users?
<--- Score

**21. How do you engage the workforce, in addition
to satisfying them?**
<--- Score

22. Are you changing as fast as the world around you?

<--- Score

23. How do you keep the momentum going?
<--- Score

24. What should you stop doing?
<--- Score

25. How important is New Product and Process Development to the user organizations mission?
<--- Score

26. Why should people listen to you?
<--- Score

27. Operational - will it work?
<--- Score

28. Do you know what you are doing? And who do you call if you don't?
<--- Score

29. Which individuals, teams or departments will be involved in New Product and Process Development?
<--- Score

30. Whose voice (department, ethnic group, women, older workers, etc) might you have missed hearing from in your company, and how might you amplify this voice to create positive momentum for your business?
<--- Score

31. If you find that you havent accomplished one of the goals for one of the steps of the New Product and

Process Development strategy, what will you do to fix it?

<--- Score

32. What New Product and Process Development skills are most important?

<--- Score

33. What information is critical to your organization that your executives are ignoring?

<--- Score

34. How do you know if you are successful?

<--- Score

35. How do you listen to customers to obtain actionable information?

<--- Score

36. If you had to rebuild your organization without any traditional competitive advantages (i.e., no killer technology, promising research, innovative product/ service delivery model, etcetera), how would your people have to approach their work and collaborate together in order to create the necessary conditions for success?

<--- Score

37. What is your BATNA (best alternative to a negotiated agreement)?

<--- Score

38. What potential megatrends could make your business model obsolete?

<--- Score

39. What are the potential basics of New Product and Process Development fraud?

<--- Score

40. What are you challenging?

<--- Score

41. How can you become more high-tech but still be high touch?

<--- Score

42. How do you cross-sell and up-sell your New Product and Process Development success?

<--- Score

43. What are the top 3 things at the forefront of your New Product and Process Development agendas for the next 3 years?

<--- Score

44. Where can you break convention?

<--- Score

45. Do you have past New Product and Process Development successes?

<--- Score

46. Are assumptions made in New Product and Process Development stated explicitly?

<--- Score

47. How do you govern and fulfill your societal responsibilities?

<--- Score

48. Is your strategy driving your strategy? Or is the

way in which you allocate resources driving your strategy?

<--- Score

49. What are specific New Product and Process Development rules to follow?

<--- Score

50. Can you maintain your growth without detracting from the factors that have contributed to your success?

<--- Score

51. What goals did you miss?

<--- Score

52. What is the funding source for this project?

<--- Score

53. What is effective New Product and Process Development?

<--- Score

54. What are the key enablers to make this New Product and Process Development move?

<--- Score

55. Are you making progress, and are you making progress as New Product and Process Development leaders?

<--- Score

56. What will be the consequences to the stakeholder (financial, reputation etc) if New Product and Process Development does not go ahead or fails to deliver the objectives?

<--- Score

57. What happens when a new employee joins the organization?
<--- Score

58. Who will determine interim and final deadlines?
<--- Score

59. What New Product and Process Development modifications can you make work for you?
<--- Score

60. What is your formula for success in New Product and Process Development ?
<--- Score

61. How do you assess the New Product and Process Development pitfalls that are inherent in implementing it?
<--- Score

62. Is New Product and Process Development dependent on the successful delivery of a current project?
<--- Score

63. How do you determine the key elements that affect New Product and Process Development workforce satisfaction, how are these elements determined for different workforce groups and segments?
<--- Score

64. What is the craziest thing you can do?
<--- Score

65. What are the gaps in your knowledge and experience?
<--- Score

66. Which New Product and Process Development goals are the most important?
<--- Score

67. How will you know that the New Product and Process Development project has been successful?
<--- Score

68. How do you make it meaningful in connecting New Product and Process Development with what users do day-to-day?
<--- Score

69. What are the barriers to increased New Product and Process Development production?
<--- Score

70. Why is it important to have senior management support for a New Product and Process Development project?
<--- Score

71. How do senior leaders deploy your organizations vision and values through your leadership system, to the workforce, to key suppliers and partners, and to customers and other stakeholders, as appropriate?
<--- Score

72. How do you foster the skills, knowledge, talents, attributes, and characteristics you want to have?

<--- Score

73. Why should you adopt a New Product and Process Development framework?
<--- Score

74. What is the range of capabilities?
<--- Score

75. What are the short and long-term New Product and Process Development goals?
<--- Score

76. What one word do you want to own in the minds of your customers, employees, and partners?
<--- Score

77. Who are four people whose careers you have enhanced?
<--- Score

78. What are the rules and assumptions your industry operates under? What if the opposite were true?
<--- Score

79. Did your employees make progress today?
<--- Score

80. Are the assumptions believable and achievable?
<--- Score

81. If you do not follow, then how to lead?
<--- Score

82. How do you maintain New Product and Process

Development's Integrity?
<--- Score

83. How is implementation research currently incorporated into each of your goals?
<--- Score

84. Which models, tools and techniques are necessary?
<--- Score

85. Who do we want your customers to become?
<--- Score

86. What is the big New Product and Process Development idea?
<--- Score

87. Is it economical; do you have the time and money?
<--- Score

88. How do you ensure that implementations of New Product and Process Development products are done in a way that ensures safety?
<--- Score

89. How do you go about securing New Product and Process Development?
<--- Score

90. Are you using a design thinking approach and integrating Innovation, New Product and Process Development Experience, and Brand Value?
<--- Score

91. Who is responsible for New Product and Process

Development?

<--- Score

92. Are all key stakeholders present at all Structured Walkthroughs?

<--- Score

93. Think of your New Product and Process Development project, what are the main functions?

<--- Score

94. Is the impact that New Product and Process Development has shown?

<--- Score

95. If your company went out of business tomorrow, would anyone who doesn't get a paycheck here care?

<--- Score

96. Do you have the right people on the bus?

<--- Score

97. What is it like to work for you?

<--- Score

98. Are you paying enough attention to the partners your company depends on to succeed?

<--- Score

99. Do you feel that more should be done in the New Product and Process Development area?

<--- Score

100. What are the long-term New Product and Process Development goals?

<--- Score

101. What must you excel at?
<--- Score

102. Is there any existing New Product and Process Development governance structure?
<--- Score

103. What are the challenges?
<--- Score

104. What are you trying to prove to yourself, and how might it be hijacking your life and business success?
<--- Score

105. Is a New Product and Process Development breakthrough on the horizon?
<--- Score

106. Who is the main stakeholder, with ultimate responsibility for driving New Product and Process Development forward?
<--- Score

107. What are the success criteria that will indicate that New Product and Process Development objectives have been met and the benefits delivered?
<--- Score

108. How much does New Product and Process Development help?
<--- Score

109. Is maximizing New Product and Process Development protection the same as minimizing New

Product and Process Development loss?
<--- Score

110. When information truly is ubiquitous, when reach and connectivity are completely global, when computing resources are infinite, and when a whole new set of impossibilities are not only possible, but happening, what will that do to your business?
<--- Score

111. What is an unauthorized commitment?
<--- Score

112. What are your most important goals for the strategic New Product and Process Development objectives?
<--- Score

113. Have benefits been optimized with all key stakeholders?
<--- Score

114. How much contingency will be available in the budget?
<--- Score

115. Has implementation been effective in reaching specified objectives so far?
<--- Score

116. What trouble can you get into?
<--- Score

117. Are you satisfied with your current role? If not, what is missing from it?

<--- Score

118. Do you have an implicit bias for capital investments over people investments?
<--- Score

119. Are you / should you be revolutionary or evolutionary?
<--- Score

120. Do you say no to customers for no reason?
<--- Score

121. Do you know who is a friend or a foe?
<--- Score

122. Do you see more potential in people than they do in themselves?
<--- Score

123. How do you manage New Product and Process Development Knowledge Management (KM)?
<--- Score

124. What does your signature ensure?
<--- Score

125. What did you miss in the interview for the worst hire you ever made?
<--- Score

126. How do you set New Product and Process Development stretch targets and how do you get people to not only participate in setting these stretch targets but also that they strive to achieve these?
<--- Score

127. Who have you, as a company, historically been when you've been at your best?
<--- Score

128. Do you think you know, or do you know you know ?
<--- Score

129. Would you rather sell to knowledgeable and informed customers or to uninformed customers?
<--- Score

130. Who do you think the world wants your organization to be?
<--- Score

131. Why not do New Product and Process Development?
<--- Score

132. Will there be any necessary staff changes (redundancies or new hires)?
<--- Score

133. Were lessons learned captured and communicated?
<--- Score

134. What may be the consequences for the performance of an organization if all stakeholders are not consulted regarding New Product and Process Development?
<--- Score

135. How do you stay inspired?

<--- Score

136. What business benefits will New Product and Process Development goals deliver if achieved?
<--- Score

137. What role does communication play in the success or failure of a New Product and Process Development project?
<--- Score

138. What is the kind of project structure that would be appropriate for your New Product and Process Development project, should it be formal and complex, or can it be less formal and relatively simple?
<--- Score

139. What do we do when new problems arise?
<--- Score

140. Who uses your product in ways you never expected?
<--- Score

141. What counts that you are not counting?
<--- Score

142. Are you maintaining a past–present–future perspective throughout the New Product and Process Development discussion?
<--- Score

143. What trophy do you want on your mantle?
<--- Score

144. If your customer were your grandmother,

would you tell her to buy what you're selling?
<--- Score

145. What is your competitive advantage?
<--- Score

146. How can you negotiate New Product and Process Development successfully with a stubborn boss, an irate client, or a deceitful coworker?
<--- Score

147. What would have to be true for the option on the table to be the best possible choice?
<--- Score

148. What projects are going on in the organization today, and what resources are those projects using from the resource pools?
<--- Score

149. How will you insure seamless interoperability of New Product and Process Development moving forward?
<--- Score

150. What threat is New Product and Process Development addressing?
<--- Score

151. What is the overall business strategy?
<--- Score

152. How do you provide a safe environment -physically and emotionally?
<--- Score

153. Who are your customers?
<--- Score

154. Are the criteria for selecting recommendations stated?
<--- Score

155. Who, on the executive team or the board, has spoken to a customer recently?
<--- Score

156. Can the schedule be done in the given time?
<--- Score

157. What relationships among New Product and Process Development trends do you perceive?
<--- Score

158. What have been your experiences in defining long range New Product and Process Development goals?
<--- Score

159. Who is on the team?
<--- Score

160. Are your responses positive or negative?
<--- Score

161. What have you done to protect your business from competitive encroachment?
<--- Score

162. What are the essentials of internal New Product and Process Development management?
<--- Score

163. How do you deal with New Product and Process Development changes?
<--- Score

164. What is the purpose of New Product and Process Development in relation to the mission?
<--- Score

165. How do you create buy-in?
<--- Score

166. Do you have enough freaky customers in your portfolio pushing you to the limit day in and day out?
<--- Score

167. What management system can you use to leverage the New Product and Process Development experience, ideas, and concerns of the people closest to the work to be done?
<--- Score

168. How long will it take to change?
<--- Score

169. Do you have the right capabilities and capacities?
<--- Score

170. How do you transition from the baseline to the target?
<--- Score

171. What happens if you do not have enough funding?
<--- Score

172. What unique value proposition (UVP) do you offer?

<--- Score

173. In retrospect, of the projects that you pulled the plug on, what percent do you wish had been allowed to keep going, and what percent do you wish had ended earlier?

<--- Score

174. What happens at your organization when people fail?

<--- Score

175. What are the performance and scale of the New Product and Process Development tools?

<--- Score

176. Who do you want your customers to become?

<--- Score

177. How do you foster innovation?

<--- Score

178. Why do and why don't your customers like your organization?

<--- Score

179. What is the source of the strategies for New Product and Process Development strengthening and reform?

<--- Score

180. How do you accomplish your long range New Product and Process Development goals?

<--- Score

181. Who else should you help?
<--- Score

182. Is the New Product and Process Development organization completing tasks effectively and efficiently?
<--- Score

183. Can you break it down?
<--- Score

184. How do you proactively clarify deliverables and New Product and Process Development quality expectations?
<--- Score

185. How do you lead with New Product and Process Development in mind?
<--- Score

186. How does New Product and Process Development integrate with other stakeholder initiatives?
<--- Score

187. Is there a work around that you can use?
<--- Score

188. What would you recommend your friend do if he/she were facing this dilemma?
<--- Score

189. What you are going to do to affect the numbers?
<--- Score

190. Whom among your colleagues do you trust, and for what?
<--- Score

191. What new services of functionality will be implemented next with New Product and Process Development ?
<--- Score

192. Political -is anyone trying to undermine this project?
<--- Score

193. What are strategies for increasing support and reducing opposition?
<--- Score

194. If you got fired and a new hire took your place, what would she do different?
<--- Score

195. What is the overall talent health of your organization as a whole at senior levels, and for each organization reporting to a member of the Senior Leadership Team?
<--- Score

196. Have new benefits been realized?
<--- Score

197. Who is responsible for ensuring appropriate resources (time, people and money) are allocated to New Product and Process Development?
<--- Score

198. Ask yourself: how would you do this work if you only had one staff member to do it?
<--- Score

199. Instead of going to current contacts for new ideas, what if you reconnected with dormant contacts--the people you used to know? If you were going reactivate a dormant tie, who would it be?
<--- Score

200. What was the last experiment you ran?
<--- Score

201. In the past year, what have you done (or could you have done) to increase the accurate perception of your company/brand as ethical and honest?
<--- Score

202. How will you motivate the stakeholders with the least vested interest?
<--- Score

203. Are there any activities that you can take off your to do list?
<--- Score

204. How do customers see your organization?
<--- Score

205. Are new benefits received and understood?
<--- Score

206. Is your basic point _____ or _____?
<--- Score

207. Do New Product and Process Development rules make a reasonable demand on a users capabilities?
<--- Score

208. Can you do all this work?
<--- Score

209. Why is New Product and Process Development important for you now?
<--- Score

210. Who will manage the integration of tools?
<--- Score

211. Which functions and people interact with the supplier and or customer?
<--- Score

212. What is a feasible sequencing of reform initiatives over time?
<--- Score

213. Is New Product and Process Development realistic, or are you setting yourself up for failure?
<--- Score

214. How will you ensure you get what you expected?
<--- Score

215. What are current New Product and Process Development paradigms?
<--- Score

Add up total points for this section:
_ _ _ _ _ = Total points for this section

Divided by: _____ (number of
statements answered) = _____
Average score for this section

Transfer your score to the New Product
and Process Development Index at the
beginning of the Self-Assessment.

New Product And Process Development and Managing Projects, Criteria for Project Managers:

1.0 Initiating Process Group: New Product And Process Development

1. Professionals want to know what is expected from them what are the deliverables?

2. Information sharing?

3. The New Product And Process Development project managers have maximum authority in which type of organization?

4. Measurable - are the targets measurable?

5. Who does what?

6. Were escalated issues resolved promptly?

7. When must it be done?

8. During which stage of Risk planning are modeling techniques used to determine overall effects of risks on New Product And Process Development project objectives for high probability, high impact risks?

9. Will the New Product And Process Development project meet the client requirements, and will it achieve the business success criteria that justified doing the New Product And Process Development project in the first place?

10. What communication items need improvement?

11. For technology New Product And Process Development projects only: Are all production

support stakeholders (Business unit, technical support, & user) prepared for implementation with appropriate contingency plans?

12. If action is called for, what form should it take?

13. How well did the chosen processes fit the needs of the New Product And Process Development project?

14. Does it make any difference if you am successful?

15. How well defined and documented were the New Product And Process Development project management processes you chose to use?

16. Realistic - are the desired results expressed in a way that the team will be motivated and believe that the required level of involvement will be obtained?

17. What were things that you did well, and could improve, and how?

18. Did you use a contractor or vendor?

19. Although the New Product And Process Development project manager does not directly manage procurement and contracting activities, who does manage procurement and contracting activities in your organization then if not the PM?

20. Who is funding the New Product And Process Development project?

1.1 Project Charter: New Product And Process Development

21. Assumptions and constraints: what assumptions were made in defining the New Product And Process Development project?

22. Where does all this information come from?

23. Strategic fit: what is the strategic initiative identifier for this New Product And Process Development project?

24. Why the improvements?

25. How high should you set your goals?

26. Why have you chosen the aim you have set forth?

27. Why do you need to manage scope?

28. What metrics could you look at?

29. What outcome, in measureable terms, are you hoping to accomplish?

30. Dependent New Product And Process Development projects: what New Product And Process Development projects must be underway or completed before this New Product And Process Development project can be successful?

31. What is the justification?

32. What is in it for you?

33. Will this replace an existing product?

34. Who ise input and support will this New Product And Process Development project require?

35. New Product And Process Development project background: what is the primary motivation for this New Product And Process Development project?

36. How will you know a change is an improvement?

37. What is the most common tool for helping define the detail?

38. What date will the task finish?

39. Assumptions: what factors, for planning purposes, are you considering to be true?

1.2 Stakeholder Register: New Product And Process Development

40. Who are the stakeholders?

41. What is the power of the stakeholder?

42. What opportunities exist to provide communications?

43. What are the major New Product And Process Development project milestones requiring communications or providing communications opportunities?

44. Who wants to talk about Security?

45. How much influence do they have on the New Product And Process Development project?

46. Who is managing stakeholder engagement?

47. How should employers make voices heard?

48. What & Why?

49. How big is the gap?

50. Is your organization ready for change?

51. How will reports be created?

1.3 Stakeholder Analysis Matrix: New Product And Process Development

52. Who will promote/support the New Product And Process Development project, provided that they are involved?

53. Who has control over whom?

54. Arena: in what fields are the actors active, where are they present?

55. What is the issue at stake?

56. What are the mechanisms of public and social accountability, and how can they be made better?

57. What tools would help you communicate?

58. Competitive advantages?

59. What is your Risk Management?

60. Usps (unique selling points)?

61. Loss of key staff?

62. What can the New Product And Process Development projects outcome be used for?

63. Advantages of proposition?

64. Beneficiaries; who are the potential beneficiaries?

65. Are you working on the right risks?

66. Guiding question: who shall you involve in the making of the stakeholder map?

67. What are innovative aspects of your organization?

68. Reputation, presence and reach?

69. What are the reimbursement requirements?

2.0 Planning Process Group: New Product And Process Development

70. What is involved in New Product And Process Development project scope management, and why is good New Product And Process Development project scope management so important on information technology New Product And Process Development projects?

71. Are you just doing busywork to pass the time?

72. How do you integrate New Product And Process Development project Planning with the Iterative/ Evolutionary SDLC?

73. What should you do next?

74. On which process should team members spend the most time?

75. How are it New Product And Process Development projects different?

76. Did the program design/ implementation strategy adequately address the planning stage necessary to set up structures, hire staff etc.?

77. What business situation is being addressed?

78. How can you make your needs known?

79. How well did the chosen processes fit the needs of

the New Product And Process Development project?

80. Is the New Product And Process Development project supported by national and/or local organizations?

81. Is the pace of implementing the products of the program ensuring the completeness of the results of the New Product And Process Development project?

82. Why do it New Product And Process Development projects fail?

83. If a task is partitionable, is this a sufficient condition to reduce the New Product And Process Development project duration?

84. Did you read it correctly?

85. To what extent have public/private national resources and/or counterparts been mobilized to contribute to the programs objective and produce results and impacts?

86. How are the principles of aid effectiveness (ownership, alignment, management for development results and mutual responsibility) being applied in the New Product And Process Development project?

87. What will you do to minimize the impact should a risk event occur?

88. You did your readings, yes?

89. What will you do?

2.1 Project Management Plan: New Product And Process Development

90. What data/reports/tools/etc. do program managers need?

91. How can you best help your organization to develop consistent practices in New Product And Process Development project management planning stages?

92. Was the peer (technical) review of the cost estimates duly coordinated with the cost estimate center of expertise and addressed in the review documentation and certification?

93. What are the training needs?

94. Is the budget realistic?

95. When is a New Product And Process Development project management plan created?

96. Who is the New Product And Process Development project Manager?

97. What does management expect of PMs?

98. What worked well?

99. Are calculations and results of analyzes essentially correct?

100. How do you organize the costs in the New Product And Process Development project management plan?

101. Are there any scope changes proposed for a previously authorized New Product And Process Development project?

102. What did not work so well?

103. What went right?

104. Who is the sponsor?

105. Are there any client staffing expectations?

106. Is there anything you would now do differently on your New Product And Process Development project based on past experience?

107. How well are you able to manage your risk?

108. Did the planning effort collaborate to develop solutions that integrate expertise, policies, programs, and New Product And Process Development projects across entities?

109. Are there any windfall benefits that would accrue to the New Product And Process Development project sponsor or other parties?

2.2 Scope Management Plan: New Product And Process Development

110. Do you document disagreements and work towards resolutions?

111. Have the procedures for identifying variances from estimates & adjusting the detailed work program been followed?

112. Is mitigation authorized or recommended?

113. Is the New Product And Process Development project sponsor clearly communicating the business case or rationale for why this New Product And Process Development project is needed?

114. Can the New Product And Process Development project team do several activities in parallel?

115. Have New Product And Process Development project management standards and procedures been identified / established and documented?

116. For which criterion is it tolerable not to meet the original parameters?

117. Do you have funding for New Product And Process Development project and product development, implementation and on-going support?

118. Has process improvement efforts been

completed before requirements efforts begin?

119. Are trade-offs between accepting the risk and mitigating the risk identified?

120. The greatest degree of uncertainty is encountered during which phase of the New Product And Process Development project life cycle?

121. Are non-critical path items updated and agreed upon with the teams?

122. What are the risks that could significantly affect the scope of the New Product And Process Development project?

123. Who is doing what for whom?

124. What strengths do you have?

125. Has a provision been made to reassess New Product And Process Development project risks at various New Product And Process Development project stages?

126. Have the key functions and capabilities been defined and assigned to each release or iteration?

127. Materials available for performing the work?

128. Are mitigation strategies identified?

2.3 Requirements Management Plan: New Product And Process Development

129. Did you distinguish the scope of work the contractor(s) will be required to do?

130. Which hardware or software, related to, or as outcome of the New Product And Process Development project is new to your organization?

131. Are all the stakeholders ready for the transition into the user community?

132. Will the product release be stable and mature enough to be deployed in the user community?

133. Did you get proper approvals?

134. How detailed should the New Product And Process Development project get?

135. How will the requirements become prioritized?

136. How knowledgeable is the team in the proposed application area?

137. Who has the authority to reject New Product And Process Development project requirements?

138. How will bidders price evaluations be done, by deliverables, phases, or in a big bang?

139. Do you have an appropriate arrangement for meetings?

140. Did you provide clear and concise specifications?

141. Are actual resource expenditures versus planned still acceptable?

142. Is the user satisfied?

143. Has the requirements team been instructed in the Change Control process?

144. Is any organizational data being used or stored?

145. Business analysis scope?

146. How will unresolved questions be handled once approval has been obtained?

147. Will the contractors involved take full responsibility?

148. Do you have an agreed upon process for alerting the New Product And Process Development project Manager if a request for change in requirements leads to a product scope change?

2.4 Requirements Documentation: New Product And Process Development

149. How linear / iterative is your Requirements Gathering process (or will it be)?

150. Can the requirement be changed without a large impact on other requirements?

151. How does what is being described meet the business need?

152. Validity. does the system provide the functions which best support the customers needs?

153. Does the system provide the functions which best support the customers needs?

154. If applicable; are there issues linked with the fact that this is an offshore New Product And Process Development project?

155. Can the requirements be checked?

156. How can you document system requirements?

157. Are there legal issues?

158. What if the system wasn t implemented?

159. Do technical resources exist?

160. Have the benefits identified with the system being identified clearly?

161. What will be the integration problems?

162. Verifiability. can the requirements be checked?

163. What happens when requirements are wrong?

164. What is the risk associated with the technology?

165. What marketing channels do you want to use: e-mail, letter or sms?

166. How much does requirements engineering cost?

167. Is the requirement properly understood?

168. What variations exist for a process?

2.5 Requirements Traceability Matrix: New Product And Process Development

169. What is the WBS?

170. Why do you manage scope?

171. Is there a requirements traceability process in place?

172. What percentage of New Product And Process Development projects are producing traceability matrices between requirements and other work products?

173. Will you use a Requirements Traceability Matrix?

174. Do you have a clear understanding of all subcontracts in place?

175. How do you manage scope?

176. Why use a WBS?

177. How small is small enough?

178. How will it affect the stakeholders personally in career?

179. What are the chronologies, contingencies, consequences, criteria?

180. Describe the process for approving requirements so they can be added to the traceability matrix and New Product And Process Development project work can be performed. Will the New Product And Process Development project requirements become approved in writing?

2.6 Project Scope Statement: New Product And Process Development

181. Did your New Product And Process Development project ask for this?

182. Will there be a Change Control Process in place?

183. Is there a process (test plans, inspections, reviews) defined for verifying outputs for each task?

184. Write a brief purpose statement for this New Product And Process Development project. Include a business justification statement. What is the product of this New Product And Process Development project?

185. Is the New Product And Process Development project organization documented and on file?

186. Were potential customers involved early in the planning process?

187. What is change?

188. Which risks does the New Product And Process Development project focus on?

189. Has the format for tracking and monitoring schedules and costs been defined?

190. What is a process you might recommend to verify the accuracy of the research deliverable?

191. Have you been able to thoroughly document the New Product And Process Development projects assumptions and constraints?

192. Elements of scope management that deal with concept development ?

193. Is there a baseline plan against which to measure progress?

194. Was planning completed before the New Product And Process Development project was initiated?

195. Is the New Product And Process Development project manager qualified and experienced in New Product And Process Development project management?

196. Have the reports to be produced, distributed, and filed been defined?

197. Is the change control process documented and on file?

198. What actions will be taken to mitigate the risk?

2.7 Assumption and Constraint Log: New Product And Process Development

199. Security analysis has access to information that is sanitized?

200. Can you perform this task or activity in a more effective manner?

201. If appropriate, is the deliverable content consistent with current New Product And Process Development project documents and in compliance with the Document Management Plan?

202. How can you prevent/fix violations?

203. How many New Product And Process Development project staff does this specific process affect?

204. Are best practices and metrics employed to identify issues, progress, performance, etc.?

205. What do you log?

206. Contradictory information between different documents?

207. Are there processes in place to ensure internal consistency between the source code components?

208. What does an audit system look like?

209. Do documented requirements exist for all critical components and areas, including technical, business, interfaces, performance, security and conversion requirements?

210. Has the approach and development strategy of the New Product And Process Development project been defined, documented and accepted by the appropriate stakeholders?

211. If it is out of compliance, should the process be amended or should the Plan be amended?

212. Are there processes in place to ensure that all the terms and code concepts have been documented consistently?

213. No superfluous information or marketing narrative?

214. Have all necessary approvals been obtained?

215. Would known impacts serve as impediments?

216. Have New Product And Process Development project management standards and procedures been established and documented?

217. What would you gain if you spent time working to improve this process?

2.8 Work Breakdown Structure: New Product And Process Development

218. When do you stop?

219. Is it still viable?

220. How far down?

221. Is the work breakdown structure (wbs) defined and is the scope of the New Product And Process Development project clear with assigned deliverable owners?

222. What is the probability of completing the New Product And Process Development project in less that xx days?

223. When does it have to be done?

224. Do you need another level?

225. Who has to do it?

226. What is the probability that the New Product And Process Development project duration will exceed xx weeks?

227. How many levels?

228. How big is a work-package?

229. Why would you develop a Work Breakdown

Structure?

230. Where does it take place?

231. How much detail?

232. Why is it useful?

233. Is it a change in scope?

2.9 WBS Dictionary: New Product And Process Development

234. Are the overhead pools formally and adequately identified?

235. Cwbs elements to be subcontracted, with identification of subcontractors?

236. What is wrong with this New Product And Process Development project?

237. Does the contractors system include procedures for measuring performance of the lowest level organization responsible for the control account?

238. Does the cost accumulation system provide for summarization of indirect costs from the point of allocation to the contract total?

239. Is cost and schedule performance measurement done in a consistent, systematic manner?

240. Is work progressively subdivided into detailed work packages as requirements are defined?

241. Can the contractor substantiate work package and planning package budgets?

242. Are procedures established to prevent changes to the contract budget base other than the already stated authorized by contractual action?

243. Are overhead costs budgets established on a basis consistent with anticipated direct business base?

244. Is all contract work included in the CWBS?

245. Contemplated overhead expenditure for each period based on the best information currently available?

246. What size should a work package be?

247. Should you include sub-activities?

248. Does the contractors system include procedures for measuring the performance of critical subcontractors?

249. Are internal budgets for authorized, and not priced changes based on the contractors resource plan for accomplishing the work?

250. Does the contractors system provide for the determination of cost variances attributable to the excess usage of material?

251. Major functional areas of contract effort?

252. Does the accounting system provide a basis for auditing records of direct costs chargeable to the contract?

2.10 Schedule Management Plan: New Product And Process Development

253. Time for overtime?

254. Are any non-compliance issues that exist due to your organizations practices communicated to your organization?

255. Are all activities logically sequenced?

256. Are the quality tools and methods identified in the Quality Plan appropriate to the New Product And Process Development project?

257. Are tasks tracked by hours?

258. Is there a Steering Committee in place?

259. Are the primary and secondary schedule tools defined?

260. Are New Product And Process Development project team members committed fulltime?

261. Are the results of quality assurance reviews provided to affected groups & individuals?

262. Are New Product And Process Development project team members involved in detailed estimating and scheduling?

263. Is there a requirements change management processes in place?

264. Will the tools selected accomplish the scheduling needs?

265. Are action items captured and managed?

266. Goal: is the schedule feasible and at what cost?

267. Are risk triggers captured?

268. Do all stakeholders know how to access this repository and where to find the New Product And Process Development project documentation?

269. Have the key elements of a coherent New Product And Process Development project management strategy been established?

270. Must the New Product And Process Development project be complete by a specified date?

271. What happens if a warning is triggered?

2.11 Activity List: New Product And Process Development

272. What is your organizations history in doing similar activities?

273. Is infrastructure setup part of your New Product And Process Development project?

274. Is there anything planned that does not need to be here?

275. What is the LF and LS for each activity?

276. Can you determine the activity that must finish, before this activity can start?

277. Are the required resources available or need to be acquired?

278. What is the probability the New Product And Process Development project can be completed in xx weeks?

279. The wbs is developed as part of a joint planning session. and how do you know that youhave done this right?

280. What are you counting on?

281. When do the individual activities need to start and finish?

282. What went well?

283. How do you determine the late start (LS) for each activity?

284. How detailed should a New Product And Process Development project get?

285. When will the work be performed?

286. For other activities, how much delay can be tolerated?

287. What went wrong?

288. What did not go as well?

289. Who will perform the work?

2.12 Activity Attributes: New Product And Process Development

290. What activity do you think you should spend the most time on?

291. Why?

292. Do you feel very comfortable with your prediction?

293. Activity: what is In the Bag?

294. Has management defined a definite timeframe for the turnaround or New Product And Process Development project window?

295. Where else does it apply?

296. How many resources do you need to complete the work scope within a limit of X number of days?

297. How do you manage time?

298. What is the general pattern here?

299. Does your organization of the data change its meaning?

300. Have you identified the Activity Leveling Priority code value on each activity?

301. Resources to accomplish the work?

302. Have constraints been applied to the start and finish milestones for the phases?

303. Would you consider either of corresponding activities an outlier?

304. What is missing?

305. Can you re-assign any activities to another resource to resolve an over-allocation?

2.13 Milestone List: New Product And Process Development

306. What specific improvements did you make to the New Product And Process Development project proposal since the previous time?

307. What background experience, skills, and strengths does the team bring to your organization?

308. Gaps in capabilities?

309. Milestone pages should display the UserID of the person who added the milestone. Does a report or query exist that provides this audit information?

310. Level of the Innovation?

311. Global influences?

312. Timescales, deadlines and pressures?

313. How late can each activity be finished and started?

314. How will you get the word out to customers?

315. Sustaining internal capabilities?

316. Environmental effects?

317. It is to be a narrative text providing the crucial aspects of your New Product And Process

Development project proposal answering what, who, how, when and where?

318. New USPs?

319. Information and research?

320. Vital contracts and partners?

321. Effects on core activities, distraction?

322. How will the milestone be verified?

323. When will the New Product And Process Development project be complete?

2.14 Network Diagram: New Product And Process Development

324. Review the logical flow of the network diagram. Take a look at which activities you have first and then sequence the activities. Do they make sense?

325. Are the required resources available?

326. What is the lowest cost to complete this New Product And Process Development project in xx weeks?

327. What to do and When?

328. What controls the start and finish of a job?

329. What job or jobs precede it?

330. Where do schedules come from?

331. What is the probability of completing the New Product And Process Development project in less that xx days?

332. What can be done concurrently?

333. What job or jobs could run concurrently?

334. Can you calculate the confidence level?

335. Will crashing x weeks return more in benefits than it costs?

336. If x is long, what would be the completion time if you break x into two parallel parts of y weeks and z weeks?

337. What activity must be completed immediately before this activity can start?

338. Planning: who, how long, what to do?

339. How difficult will it be to do specific activities on this New Product And Process Development project?

340. Are you on time?

341. What activities must occur simultaneously with this activity?

2.15 Activity Resource Requirements: New Product And Process Development

342. Organizational Applicability?

343. Do you use tools like decomposition and rolling-wave planning to produce the activity list and other outputs?

344. Are there unresolved issues that need to be addressed?

345. Other support in specific areas?

346. What is the Work Plan Standard?

347. Why do you do that?

348. How do you handle petty cash?

349. Anything else?

350. When does monitoring begin?

351. How many signatures do you require on a check and does this match what is in your policy and procedures?

352. What are constraints that you might find during the Human Resource Planning process?

353. Which logical relationship does the PDM use

most often?

2.16 Resource Breakdown Structure: New Product And Process Development

354. Who needs what information?

355. Who will be used as a New Product And Process Development project team member?

356. Is predictive resource analysis being done?

357. Who is allowed to perform which functions?

358. What is the primary purpose of the human resource plan?

359. The list could probably go on, but, the thing that you would most like to know is, How long & How much?

360. How can this help you with team building?

361. What defines a successful New Product And Process Development project?

362. Who will use the system?

363. Goals for the New Product And Process Development project. What is each stakeholders desired outcome for the New Product And Process Development project?

364. Any changes from stakeholders?

365. What are the requirements for resource data?

366. Which resources should be in the resource pool?

367. Who is allowed to see what data about which resources?

2.17 Activity Duration Estimates: New Product And Process Development

368. Briefly summarize the work done by Maslow, Herzberg, McClellan, McGregor, Ouchi, Thamhain and Wilemon, and Covey. How do theories relate to New Product And Process Development project management?

369. Why is it important to determine activity sequencing on New Product And Process Development projects?

370. Do you think many other organizations could apply this methodology, or does each organization need to create its own methodology?

371. Which would be the NEXT thing for the New Product And Process Development project manager to do?

372. Does the case present a realistic scenario?

373. Why should New Product And Process Development project managers strive to make jobs look easy?

374. What does it mean to take a systems view of a New Product And Process Development project?

375. Can they use the already stated?

376. What are some general rules of thumb for

deciding if cost variance, schedule variance, cost performance index, and schedule performance index numbers are good or bad?

377. How can organizations use a weighted decision matrix to evaluate proposals as part of source selection?

378. Write a oneto two-page paper describing your dream team for this New Product And Process Development project. What type of people would you want on your team?

379. Is a New Product And Process Development project charter created once a New Product And Process Development project is formally recognized?

380. Are processes defined to monitor New Product And Process Development project cost and schedule variances?

381. Why is there a growing trend in outsourcing, especially in the government?

382. Are procedures followed to ensure information is available to stakeholders in a timely manner?

383. Total slack can be calculated by which equations?

384. What is the critical path for this New Product And Process Development project and how long is it?

385. Are adjustments implemented to correct or prevent defects?

386. Why do you need a good WBS to use New

Product And Process Development project management software?

387. Who will be the main sponsor for it?

2.18 Duration Estimating Worksheet: New Product And Process Development

388. What is an Average New Product And Process Development project?

389. What utility impacts are there?

390. How should ongoing costs be monitored to try to keep the New Product And Process Development project within budget?

391. How can the New Product And Process Development project be displayed graphically to better visualize the activities?

392. What is your role?

393. Will the New Product And Process Development project collaborate with the local community and leverage resources?

394. Why estimate costs?

395. Does the New Product And Process Development project provide innovative ways for stakeholders to overcome obstacles or deliver better outcomes?

396. What is next?

397. Can the New Product And Process Development project be constructed as planned?

398. Done before proceeding with this activity or what can be done concurrently?

399. Value pocket identification & quantification what are value pockets?

400. Define the work as completely as possible. What work will be included in the New Product And Process Development project?

401. What is cost and New Product And Process Development project cost management?

402. Do any colleagues have experience with your organization and/or RFPs?

403. What work will be included in the New Product And Process Development project?

404. What info is needed?

405. What are the critical bottleneck activities?

2.19 Project Schedule: New Product And Process Development

406. Eliminate unnecessary activities. Are there activities that came from a template or previous New Product And Process Development project that are not applicable on this phase of this New Product And Process Development project?

407. What is the most mis-scheduled part of process?

408. Is the New Product And Process Development project schedule available for all New Product And Process Development project team members to review?

409. Is the structure for tracking the New Product And Process Development project schedule well defined and assigned to a specific individual?

410. Should you have a test for each code module?

411. What is the purpose of a New Product And Process Development project schedule?

412. What is the difference?

413. To what degree is do you feel the entire team was committed to the New Product And Process Development project schedule?

414. Are quality inspections and review activities listed in the New Product And Process Development

project schedule(s)?

415. Is there a Schedule Management Plan that establishes the criteria and activities for developing, monitoring and controlling the New Product And Process Development project schedule?

416. Why or why not?

417. How do you manage New Product And Process Development project Risk?

418. Are key risk mitigation strategies added to the New Product And Process Development project schedule?

419. How can you shorten the schedule?

420. Are activities connected because logic dictates the order in which others occur?

421. Are all remaining durations correct?

422. How closely did the initial New Product And Process Development project Schedule compare with the actual schedule?

423. What does that mean?

2.20 Cost Management Plan: New Product And Process Development

424. Is an industry recognized mechanized support tool(s) being used for New Product And Process Development project scheduling & tracking?

425. What are the nine areas of expertise?

426. Are parking lot items captured?

427. Have process improvement efforts been completed before requirements efforts begin?

428. Were the budget estimates reasonable?

429. Is it possible to track all classes of New Product And Process Development project work (e.g. scheduled, un-scheduled, defect repair, etc.)?

430. Scope of work – What is the scope of work for each of the planned contracts?

431. Have the procedures for identifying budget variances been followed?

432. Does the New Product And Process Development project have a Statement of Work?

433. Are post milestone New Product And Process Development project reviews (PMPR) conducted with your organization at least once a year?

434. The definition of the New Product And Process Development project scope what needs to be accomplished?

435. Has New Product And Process Development project success criteria been defined?

436. Is a payment system in place with proper reviews and approvals?

437. Has a provision been made to reassess New Product And Process Development project risks at various New Product And Process Development project stages?

438. Are internal New Product And Process Development project status meetings held at reasonable intervals?

439. Planning and scheduling responsibilities – How will the responsibilities for planning and scheduling be allocated?

440. How difficult will it be to do specific tasks on the New Product And Process Development project?

441. Responsibilities – what is the split of responsibilities between the owner and contractors?

442. Quality assurance overheads?

2.21 Activity Cost Estimates: New Product And Process Development

443. Were the tasks or work products prepared by the consultant useful?

444. Specific - is the objective clear in terms of what, how, when, and where the situation will be changed?

445. What makes a good activity description?

446. Were you satisfied with the work?

447. How do you fund change orders?

448. The impact and what actions were taken?

449. Were the costs or charges reasonable?

450. Where can you get activity reports?

451. Who determines the quality and expertise of contractors?

452. Did the New Product And Process Development project team have the right skills?

453. How Award?

454. Eac -estimate at completion, what is the total job expected to cost?

455. How do you manage cost?

456. What is the New Product And Process Development projects sustainability strategy that will ensure New Product And Process Development project results will endure or be sustained?

457. Certification of actual expenditures?

458. What is the activity inventory?

459. What is procurement?

2.22 Cost Estimating Worksheet: New Product And Process Development

460. Does the New Product And Process Development project provide innovative ways for stakeholders to overcome obstacles or deliver better outcomes?

461. Who is best positioned to know and assist in identifying corresponding factors?

462. Can a trend be established from historical performance data on the selected measure and are the criteria for using trend analysis or forecasting methods met?

463. How will the results be shared and to whom?

464. What can be included?

465. What will others want?

466. What is the purpose of estimating?

467. What is the estimated labor cost today based upon this information?

468. Will the New Product And Process Development project collaborate with the local community and leverage resources?

469. Is it feasible to establish a control group arrangement?

470. Ask: are others positioned to know, are others credible, and will others cooperate?

471. What happens to any remaining funds not used?

472. Identify the timeframe necessary to monitor progress and collect data to determine how the selected measure has changed?

473. What costs are to be estimated?

474. What additional New Product And Process Development project(s) could be initiated as a result of this New Product And Process Development project?

475. Is the New Product And Process Development project responsive to community need?

2.23 Cost Baseline: New Product And Process Development

476. Vac -variance at completion, how much over/ under budget do you expect to be?

477. What deliverables come first?

478. What would the life cycle costs be?

479. On time?

480. Has the New Product And Process Development project documentation been archived or otherwise disposed as described in the New Product And Process Development project communication plan?

481. Is the cr within New Product And Process Development project scope?

482. Will the New Product And Process Development project fail if the change request is not executed?

483. Is there anything you need from upper management in order to be successful?

484. What do you want to measure ?

485. Review your risk triggers -have your risks changed?

486. Have all approved changes to the New Product And Process Development project requirement been

identified and impact on the performance, cost, and schedule baselines documented?

487. How accurate do cost estimates need to be?

488. Who will use corresponding metrics ?

489. Are procedures defined by which the cost baseline may be changed?

490. Have all the product or service deliverables been accepted by the customer?

491. Should a more thorough impact analysis be conducted?

492. Has the documentation relating to operation and maintenance of the product(s) or service(s) been delivered to, and accepted by, operations management?

493. Why do you manage cost?

494. What is the most important thing to do next to make your New Product And Process Development project successful?

2.24 Quality Management Plan: New Product And Process Development

495. Has a New Product And Process Development project Communications Plan been developed?

496. How are corresponding standards measured?

497. How does your organization make it easy for customers to seek assistance or complain?

498. How are new requirements or changes to requirements identified?

499. Results Available?

500. What are the established criteria that sampling / testing data are compared against?

501. Are you following the quality standards?

502. Can it be done better?

503. Modifications to the requirements?

504. Would impacts defined serve as impediments?

505. How does training support what is important to your organization and the individual?

506. How many New Product And Process Development project staff does this specific process affect?

507. How long do you retain data?

508. Is the amount of effort justified by the anticipated value of forming a new process?

509. How do you ensure that your sampling methods and procedures meet your data quality objectives?

510. Have all involved stakeholders and work groups committed to the New Product And Process Development project?

511. When reporting to different audiences, do you vary the form or type of report?

512. Were there any deficiencies / issues identified in the prior years self-assessment?

513. Are there trends or hot spots?

2.25 Quality Metrics: New Product And Process Development

514. Who notifies stakeholders of normal and abnormal results?

515. Were number of defects identified?

516. Was the overall quality better or worse than previous products?

517. Is there a set of procedures to capture, analyze and act on quality metrics?

518. Which data do others need in one place to target areas of improvement?

519. When is the security analysis testing complete?

520. Can you correlate your quality metrics to profitability?

521. Has it met internal or external standards?

522. Was material distributed on time?

523. How do you calculate corresponding metrics?

524. Where did complaints, returns and warranty claims come from?

525. Can visual measures help you to filter visualizations of interest?

526. What percentage are outcome-based?

527. How do you know if everyone is trying to improve the right things?

528. What level of statistical confidence do you use?

529. What happens if you get an abnormal result?

530. What method of measurement do you use?

531. Did evaluation start on time?

532. Are quality metrics defined?

533. What metrics are important and most beneficial to measure?

2.26 Process Improvement Plan: New Product And Process Development

534. What lessons have you learned so far?

535. Who should prepare the process improvement action plan?

536. Are you making progress on the goals?

537. How do you measure?

538. How do you manage quality?

539. Management commitment at all levels?

540. What personnel are the champions for the initiative?

541. What personnel are the coaches for your initiative?

542. What actions are needed to address the problems and achieve the goals?

543. Where are you now?

544. Where do you want to be?

545. Purpose of goal: the motive is determined by asking, why do you want to achieve this goal?

546. Have the supporting tools been developed or

acquired?

547. What is the return on investment?

548. Why do you want to achieve the goal?

549. Are you meeting the quality standards?

550. What is quality and how will you ensure it?

551. Are you making progress on the improvement framework?

2.27 Responsibility Assignment Matrix: New Product And Process Development

552. Wbs elements contractually specified for reporting of status (lowest level only)?

553. Are the wbs and organizational levels for application of the New Product And Process Development projected overhead costs identified?

554. Too many as: does a proper segregation of duties exist?

555. The total budget for the contract (including estimates for authorized and unpriced work)?

556. What is the purpose of assigning and documenting responsibility?

557. What travel needed?

558. What happens when others get pulled for higher priority New Product And Process Development projects?

559. What are the deliverables?

560. Changes in the overhead pool and/or organization structures?

561. What does wbs accomplish?

562. Are control accounts opened and closed based on the start and completion of work contained therein?

563. All cwbs elements specified for external reporting?

564. How many hours by each staff member/rate?

565. Are records maintained to show how undistributed budgets are controlled?

566. Time-phased control account budgets?

567. Evaluate the performance of operating organizations?

568. Are all elements of indirect expense identified to overhead cost budgets of New Product And Process Development projections?

569. Are your organizations and items of cost assigned to each pool identified?

2.28 Roles and Responsibilities: New Product And Process Development

570. To decide whether to use a quality measurement, ask how will you know when it is achieved?

571. What should you do now to ensure that you are exceeding expectations and excelling in your current position?

572. Are New Product And Process Development project team roles and responsibilities identified and documented?

573. Concern: where are you limited or have no authority, where you can not influence?

574. Who is responsible for implementation activities and where will the functions, roles and responsibilities be defined?

575. What areas of supervision are challenging for you?

576. What should you highlight for improvement?

577. Does your vision/mission support a culture of quality data?

578. Are your budgets supportive of a culture of quality data?

579. Was the expectation clearly communicated?

580. Where are you most strong as a supervisor?

581. What expectations were NOT met?

582. Who is responsible for each task?

583. Authority: what areas/New Product And Process Development projects in your work do you have the authority to decide upon and act on the already stated decisions?

584. Have you ever been a part of this team?

585. What should you do now to prepare for your career 5+ years from now?

586. Required skills, knowledge, experience?

587. Be specific; avoid generalities. Thank you and great work alone are insufficient. What exactly do you appreciate and why?

588. Key conclusions and recommendations: Are conclusions and recommendations relevant and acceptable?

589. Do the values and practices inherent in the culture of your organization foster or hinder the process?

2.29 Human Resource Management Plan: New Product And Process Development

590. Is your organization primarily focused on a specific industry?

591. Who needs training?

592. How to convince employees that this is a necessary process?

593. Are all resource assumptions documented?

594. Are all vendor contracts closed out?

595. How well does your organization communicate?

596. How do you determine what key skills and talents are needed to meet the objectives. Is your organization primarily focused on a specific industry?

597. Does the New Product And Process Development project have a Quality Culture?

598. Personnel with expertise?

599. Have New Product And Process Development project team accountabilities & responsibilities been clearly defined?

600. Is the steering committee active in New Product And Process Development project oversight?

601. Are the people assigned to the New Product And Process Development project sufficiently qualified?

602. Alignment to strategic goals & objectives?

603. Are target dates established for each milestone deliverable?

604. Is this New Product And Process Development project carried out in partnership with other groups/ organizations?

605. Has the budget been baselined?

606. Who are the people that make up your organization and whom create the success that your organization enjoys as a whole?

2.30 Communications Management Plan: New Product And Process Development

607. Which team member will work with each stakeholder?

608. Where do team members get information?

609. What to learn?

610. Will messages be directly related to the release strategy or phases of the New Product And Process Development project?

611. Which stakeholders are thought leaders, influences, or early adopters?

612. What approaches to you feel are the best ones to use?

613. Conflict resolution -which method when?

614. How did the term stakeholder originate?

615. Who have you worked with in past, similar initiatives?

616. Do you feel a register helps?

617. Why do you manage communications?

618. Who did you turn to if you had questions?

619. What approaches do you use?

620. Is the stakeholder role recognized by your organization?

621. Do you feel more overwhelmed by stakeholders?

622. How do you manage communications?

623. Are there common objectives between the team and the stakeholder?

624. What is the stakeholders level of authority?

625. Are there potential barriers between the team and the stakeholder?

2.31 Risk Management Plan: New Product And Process Development

626. How is risk identification performed?

627. Are New Product And Process Development project requirements stable?

628. Does the software engineering team have the right mix of skills?

629. What does a risk management program do?

630. How can you fix it?

631. Do requirements put excessive performance constraints on the product?

632. Why is product liability a serious issue?

633. Are the required plans included, such as nonstructural flood risk management plans?

634. What can go wrong?

635. Litigation – what is the probability that lawsuits will cause problems or delays in the New Product And Process Development project?

636. Why do you want risk management?

637. Is the process being followed?

638. Are staff committed for the duration of the product?

639. Which risks should get the attention?

640. What should be done with non-critical risks?

641. Do you have a consistent repeatable process that is actually used?

642. Are testing tools available and suitable?

643. Does the customer have a solid idea of what is required?

644. Who has experience with this?

645. Is there additional information that would make you more confident about your analysis?

2.32 Risk Register: New Product And Process Development

646. Risk probability and impact: how will the probabilities and impacts of risk items be assessed?

647. What should you do now?

648. What has changed since the last period?

649. What may happen or not go according to plan?

650. Recovery actions - planned actions taken once a risk has occurred to allow you to move on. What should you do after?

651. What further options might be available for responding to the risk?

652. What are you going to do to limit the New Product And Process Development projects risk exposure due to the identified risks?

653. What is the appropriate level of risk management for this New Product And Process Development project?

654. What action, if any, has been taken to respond to the risk?

655. Assume the risk event or situation happens, what would the impact be?

656. How could corresponding Risk affect the New Product And Process Development project in terms of cost and schedule?

657. Preventative actions - planned actions to reduce the likelihood a risk will occur and/or reduce the seriousness should it occur. What should you do now?

658. Assume the event happens, what is the Most Likely impact?

659. What is your current and future risk profile?

660. User involvement: do you have the right users?

661. Can the likelihood and impact of failing to achieve corresponding recommendations and action plans be assessed?

662. What should you do when?

663. What risks might negatively or positively affect achieving the New Product And Process Development project objectives?

664. Severity Prediction?

2.33 Probability and Impact Assessment: New Product And Process Development

665. What risks are necessary to achieve success?

666. What are its business ethics?

667. How do the products attain the specifications?

668. Are enough people available?

669. Is the customer willing to commit significant time to the requirements gathering process?

670. Are the software tools integrated with each other?

671. What new technologies are being explored in the same area?

672. What is the probability of the risk occurring?

673. How completely has the customer been identified?

674. Are flexibility and reuse paramount?

675. What are the preparations required for facing difficulties?

676. How do you define a risk?

677. Are the best people available?

678. Do you train all developers in the process?

679. Who are the international/overseas New Product And Process Development project partners (equipment supplier/supplier/consultant/contractor) for this New Product And Process Development project?

680. Is the delay in one subNew Product And Process Development project going to affect another?

681. How risk averse are you?

682. Which role do you have in the New Product And Process Development project?

683. Are New Product And Process Development project requirements stable?

2.34 Probability and Impact Matrix: New Product And Process Development

684. What are the probable external agencies to act as New Product And Process Development project manager?

685. Have you ascribed a level of confidence to every critical technical objective?

686. What will be the environmental impact of the New Product And Process Development project?

687. Are people attending meetings and doing work?

688. Has the need for the New Product And Process Development project been properly established?

689. How would you suggest monitoring for risk transition indicators?

690. How solid are the price-volume New Product And Process Development projections?

691. Why do you need to manage New Product And Process Development project Risk?

692. What are the methods to deal with risks?

693. What is the culture of the market and your organization?

694. What needs to be DONE?

695. Is New Product And Process Development project scope stable?

696. How much risk do others need to take?

697. Which is the BEST thing to do?

698. What is the risk appetite?

699. Prioritized components/features?

700. My New Product And Process Development project leader has suddenly left your organization, what do you do?

2.35 Risk Data Sheet: New Product And Process Development

701. What if client refuses?

702. What is the chance that it will happen?

703. What will be the consequences if it happens?

704. What was measured?

705. How can hazards be reduced?

706. What will be the consequences if the risk happens?

707. If it happens, what are the consequences?

708. What are your core values?

709. Has a sensitivity analysis been carried out?

710. What are the main opportunities available to you that you should grab while you can?

711. Whom do you serve (customers)?

712. How reliable is the data source?

713. Type of risk identified?

714. Are new hazards created?

715. What are you weak at and therefore need to do better?

716. Potential for recurrence?

717. How can it happen?

718. What actions can be taken to eliminate or remove risk?

719. During work activities could hazards exist?

2.36 Procurement Management Plan: New Product And Process Development

720. Has a structured approach been used to break work effort into manageable components (WBS)?

721. Is the New Product And Process Development project schedule available for all New Product And Process Development project team members to review?

722. Is there a formal set of procedures supporting Issues Management?

723. Are New Product And Process Development project team members committed fulltime?

724. Is there general agreement & acceptance of the current status and progress of the New Product And Process Development project?

725. Are schedule deliverables actually delivered?

726. Are governance roles and responsibilities documented?

727. Was the scope definition used in task sequencing?

728. Are decisions made in a timely manner?

729. Financial capacity; does the seller have, or can

the seller reasonably be expected to obtain, the financial resources needed?

730. Have the key elements of a coherent New Product And Process Development project management strategy been established?

731. Is there an approved case?

732. In which phase of the Acquisition Process Cycle does source qualifications reside?

733. How will multiple providers be managed?

734. Is the New Product And Process Development project sponsor clearly communicating the business case or rationale for why this New Product And Process Development project is needed?

735. Are post milestone New Product And Process Development project reviews (PMPR) conducted with your organization at least once a year?

2.37 Source Selection Criteria: New Product And Process Development

736. How can business terms and conditions be improved to yield more effective price competition?

737. Who is entitled to a debriefing?

738. With the rapid changes in information technology, will media be readable in five or ten years?

739. How should comments received in response to a RFP be handled?

740. What are the special considerations for preaward debriefings?

741. Do you consider all weaknesses, significant weaknesses, and deficiencies?

742. What aspects should the contracting officer brief the New Product And Process Development project on prior to evaluation of proposals?

743. What past performance information should be requested?

744. Can you make a cost/technical tradeoff?

745. How will you evaluate offerors proposals?

746. Has all proposal data been loaded?

747. When is it appropriate to conduct a preproposal conference?

748. What instructions should be provided regarding oral presentations?

749. Can you prevent comparison of proposals?

750. Does your documentation identify why the team concurs or differs with reported performance from past performance report (CPARs, questionnaire responses, etc.)?

751. Comparison of each offers prices to the estimated prices -are there significant differences?

752. What information is to be provided and when should it be provided?

753. What are open book debriefings?

754. What is the last item a New Product And Process Development project manager must do to finalize New Product And Process Development project close-out?

755. Can you reasonably estimate total organization requirements for the coming year?

2.38 Stakeholder Management Plan: New Product And Process Development

756. Is a pmo (New Product And Process Development project management office) in place and does it provide oversight to the New Product And Process Development project?

757. Are estimating assumptions and constraints captured?

758. Have you eliminated all duplicative tasks or manual efforts, where appropriate?

759. Are staff skills known and available for each task?

760. Is there an issues management plan in place?

761. Are procurement deliverables arriving on time and to specification?

762. Have all stakeholders been identified?

763. Which risks pose the highest threat?

764. What are the criteria for selecting other suppliers, including subcontractors?

765. Do you use diagrams and tables to account for complex concepts and increase overall readability?

766. Do any protocols apply for records management?

767. Detail warranty and/or maintenance periods?

768. Are metrics used to evaluate and manage Vendors?

769. Who will the report(s) be delivered to?

2.39 Change Management Plan: New Product And Process Development

770. Who will fund the training?

771. What tasks are needed?

772. Is there an adequate supply of people for the new roles?

773. Who will be the change levers?

774. Are there any restrictions on who can receive the communications?

775. Clearly articulate the overall business benefits of the New Product And Process Development project -why are you doing this now?

776. What would be an estimate of the total cost for the activities required to carry out the change initiative?

777. Identify the risk and assess the significance and likelihood of it occurring and plan the contingency What risks may occur upfront?

778. How will the stakeholders share information and transfer knowledge?

779. What prerequisite knowledge or training is required?

780. What prerequisite knowledge do corresponding groups need?

781. What is the negative impact of communicating too soon or too late?

782. Readiness -what is a successful end state?

783. What provokes organizational change?

784. What are the needs, priorities and special interests of the audience?

785. What new roles are needed?

786. What risks may occur upfront, during implementation and after implementation?

787. Who will do the training?

788. Will a different work structure focus people on what is important?

3.0 Executing Process Group: New Product And Process Development

789. What is the shortest possible time it will take to complete this New Product And Process Development project?

790. What areas does the group agree are the biggest success on the New Product And Process Development project?

791. Is the New Product And Process Development project performing better or worse than planned?

792. How does a New Product And Process Development project life cycle differ from a product life cycle?

793. In what way has the program come up with innovative measures for problem-solving?

794. How do you prevent staff are just doing busywork to pass the time?

795. How many different communication channels does the New Product And Process Development project team have?

796. Have operating capacities been created and/or reinforced in partners?

797. How can your organization use a weighted decision matrix to evaluate proposals as part of

source selection?

798. How can you use Microsoft New Product And Process Development project and Excel to assist in New Product And Process Development project risk management?

799. What good practices or successful experiences or transferable examples have been identified?

800. When will the New Product And Process Development project be done?

801. What type of information goes in the quality assurance plan?

802. What is the critical path for this New Product And Process Development project and how long is it?

803. Is the New Product And Process Development project making progress in helping to achieve the set results?

804. Are the necessary foundations in place to ensure the sustainability of the results of the programme?

805. Who will be the main sponsor?

806. How do you enter durations, link tasks, and view critical path information?

3.1 Team Member Status Report: New Product And Process Development

807. Are the products of your organizations New Product And Process Development projects meeting customers objectives?

808. Will the staff do training or is that done by a third party?

809. Does every department have to have a New Product And Process Development project Manager on staff?

810. Are the attitudes of staff regarding New Product And Process Development project work improving?

811. Is there evidence that staff is taking a more professional approach toward management of your organizations New Product And Process Development projects?

812. Does your organization have the means (staff, money, contract, etc.) to produce or to acquire the product, good, or service?

813. Do you have an Enterprise New Product And Process Development project Management Office (EPMO)?

814. What specific interest groups do you have in place?

815. The problem with Reward & Recognition Programs is that the truly deserving people all too often get left out. How can you make it practical?

816. Are your organizations New Product And Process Development projects more successful over time?

817. How does this product, good, or service meet the needs of the New Product And Process Development project and your organization as a whole?

818. When a teams productivity and success depend on collaboration and the efficient flow of information, what generally fails them?

819. Does the product, good, or service already exist within your organization?

820. What is to be done?

821. How much risk is involved?

822. How will resource planning be done?

823. Why is it to be done?

824. How can you make it practical?

825. How it is to be done?

3.2 Change Request: New Product And Process Development

826. Are there requirements attributes that can discriminate between high and low reliability?

827. How are the measures for carrying out the change established?

828. How fast will change requests be approved?

829. Who is responsible to authorize changes?

830. What is the purpose of change control?

831. Are there requirements attributes that are strongly related to the occurrence of defects and failures?

832. How shall the implementation of changes be recorded?

833. What has an inspector to inspect and to check?

834. What is the function of the change control committee?

835. Are change requests logged and managed?

836. What mechanism is used to appraise others of changes that are made?

837. Who needs to approve change requests?

838. Who is included in the change control team?

839. What must be taken into consideration when introducing change control programs?

840. Will this change conflict with other requirements changes (e.g., lead to conflicting operational scenarios)?

841. Are you implementing itil processes?

842. How can changes be graded?

843. Which requirements attributes affect the risk to reliability the most?

844. How can you ensure that changes have been made properly?

845. Are there requirements attributes that are strongly related to the complexity and size?

3.3 Change Log: New Product And Process Development

846. Will the New Product And Process Development project fail if the change request is not executed?

847. How does this change affect scope?

848. How does this relate to the standards developed for specific business processes?

849. Who initiated the change request?

850. Is the submitted change a new change or a modification of a previously approved change?

851. Is the change backward compatible without limitations?

852. Is this a mandatory replacement?

853. When was the request approved?

854. Is the requested change request a result of changes in other New Product And Process Development project(s)?

855. Is the change request within New Product And Process Development project scope?

856. Where do changes come from?

857. Does the suggested change request seem to

represent a necessary enhancement to the product?

858. Is the change request open, closed or pending?

859. How does this change affect the timeline of the schedule?

860. When was the request submitted?

861. Do the described changes impact on the integrity or security of the system?

862. Does the suggested change request represent a desired enhancement to the products functionality?

3.4 Decision Log: New Product And Process Development

863. How consolidated and comprehensive a story can you tell by capturing currently available incident data in a central location and through a log of key decisions during an incident?

864. Behaviors; what are guidelines that the team has identified that will assist them with getting the most out of team meetings?

865. It becomes critical to track and periodically revisit both operational effectiveness; Are you noticing all that you need to, and are you interpreting what you see effectively?

866. With whom was the decision shared or considered?

867. What is the line where eDiscovery ends and document review begins?

868. How does an increasing emphasis on cost containment influence the strategies and tactics used?

869. What are the cost implications?

870. Is everything working as expected?

871. Who is the decisionmaker?

872. Adversarial environment. is your opponent open to a non-traditional workflow, or will it likely challenge anything you do?

873. Does anything need to be adjusted?

874. Do strategies and tactics aimed at less than full control reduce the costs of management or simply shift the cost burden?

875. What makes you different or better than others companies selling the same thing?

876. Linked to original objective?

877. What was the rationale for the decision?

878. How does provision of information, both in terms of content and presentation, influence acceptance of alternative strategies?

879. Is your opponent open to a non-traditional workflow, or will it likely challenge anything you do?

880. What is your overall strategy for quality control / quality assurance procedures?

881. How do you define success?

882. What alternatives/risks were considered?

3.5 Quality Audit: New Product And Process Development

883. How does your organization know that its system for managing intellectual property issues is appropriately effective, constructive and fair?

884. How does your organization know that its Strategic Plan is providing the best guidance for the future of your organization?

885. How does your organization know that its policy management system is appropriately effective and constructive?

886. Are complaint files maintained?

887. Are people allowed to contribute ideas?

888. Are all staff empowered and encouraged to contribute to ongoing improvement efforts?

889. How does your organization know that its system for attending to the particular needs of its international staff is appropriately effective and constructive?

890. Does the audit organization have experience in performing the required work for entities of your type and size?

891. How well do you think your organization engages with the outside community?

892. Does the report read coherently?

893. How does your organization know that the quality of its supervisors is appropriately effective and constructive?

894. Is there a written corporate quality policy?

895. Are all employees made aware of device defects which may occur from the improper performance of specific jobs?

896. Is there any content that may be legally actionable?

897. How does your organization ensure that equipment is appropriately maintained and producing valid results?

898. How does your organization know that its relationships with relevant professional bodies are appropriately effective and constructive?

899. How does your organization know that its quality of teaching is appropriately effective and constructive?

900. How does your organization know that its staff have appropriate access to a fair and effective grievance process?

901. How does your organization know that its research funding systems are appropriately effective and constructive in enabling quality research outcomes?

902. How does your organization know that its staff are presenting original work, and properly acknowledging the work of others?

3.6 Team Directory: New Product And Process Development

903. Why is the work necessary?

904. Do purchase specifications and configurations match requirements?

905. How does the team resolve conflicts and ensure tasks are completed?

906. Process decisions: is work progressing on schedule and per contract requirements?

907. Who will talk to the customer?

908. Process decisions: are there any statutory or regulatory issues relevant to the timely execution of work?

909. Who are your stakeholders (customers, sponsors, end users, team members)?

910. What needs to be communicated?

911. How do unidentified risks impact the outcome of the New Product And Process Development project?

912. Who should receive information (all stakeholders)?

913. How and in what format should information be presented?

914. What are you going to deliver or accomplish?

915. How will you accomplish and manage the objectives?

916. Decisions: is the most suitable form of contract being used?

917. Does a New Product And Process Development project team directory list all resources assigned to the New Product And Process Development project?

918. Timing: when do the effects of communication take place?

919. Contract requirements complied with?

920. Who are the Team Members?

921. Process decisions: which organizational elements and which individuals will be assigned management functions?

3.7 Team Operating Agreement: New Product And Process Development

922. How will your group handle planned absences?

923. Do you ask participants to close laptops and place mobile devices on silent on the table while the meeting is in progress?

924. Do you ensure that all participants know how to use the required technology?

925. How will you divide work equitably?

926. Confidentiality: how will confidential information be handled?

927. What is the number of cases currently teamed?

928. Did you determine the technology methods that best match the messages to be communicated?

929. Has the appropriate access to relevant data and analysis capability been granted?

930. What is culture?

931. Do you determine the meeting length and time of day?

932. Do you solicit member feedback about meetings and what would make them better?

933. How do you want to be thought of and known within your organization?

934. Do you leverage technology engagement tools group chat, polls, screen sharing, etc.?

935. Are there more than two functional areas represented by your team?

936. Communication protocols: how will the team communicate?

937. Do team members need to frequently communicate as a full group to make timely decisions?

938. What resources can be provided for the team in terms of equipment, space, time for training, protected time and space for meetings, and travel allowances?

939. Methodologies: how will key team processes be implemented, such as training, research, work deliverable production, review and approval processes, knowledge management, and meeting procedures?

940. What is the anticipated procedure (recruitment, solicitation of volunteers, or assignment) for selecting team members?

3.8 Team Performance Assessment: New Product And Process Development

941. To what degree does the teams work approach provide opportunity for members to engage in fact-based problem solving?

942. How much interpersonal friction is there in your team?

943. Effects of crew composition on crew performance: Does the whole equal the sum of its parts?

944. To what degree are the teams goals and objectives clear, simple, and measurable?

945. To what degree are sub-teams possible or necessary?

946. To what degree can team members meet frequently enough to accomplish the teams ends?

947. To what degree does the teams purpose contain themes that are particularly meaningful and memorable?

948. Can team performance be reliably measured in simulator and live exercises using the same assessment tool?

949. To what degree is the team cognizant of small

wins to be celebrated along the way?

950. What is method variance?

951. When a reviewer complains about method variance, what is the essence of the complaint?

952. When does the medium matter?

953. To what degree will the team adopt a concrete, clearly understood, and agreed-upon approach that will result in achievement of the teams goals?

954. To what degree are the goals ambitious?

955. To what degree are fresh input and perspectives systematically caught and added (for example, through information and analysis, new members, and senior sponsors)?

956. To what degree are staff involved as partners in the improvement process?

957. To what degree do team members understand one anothers roles and skills?

958. How do you encourage members to learn from each other?

959. Delaying market entry: how long is too long?

960. Individual task proficiency and team process behavior: what is important for team functioning?

3.9 Team Member Performance Assessment: New Product And Process Development

961. What are best practices in use for the performance measurement system?

962. To what degree can the team measure progress against specific goals?

963. Are the draft goals SMART ?

964. What steps have you taken to improve performance?

965. What types of learning are targeted (e.g., cognitive, affective, psychomotor, procedural)?

966. How do you create a self-sustaining capacity for a collaborative culture?

967. Does the rater (supervisor) have to wait for the interim or final performance assessment review to tell an employee that the employees performance is unsatisfactory?

968. What is needed for effective data teams?

969. To what degree are the relative importance and priority of the goals clear to all team members?

970. Which training platform formats (i.e., mobile, virtual, videogame-based) were implemented in your

effort(s)?

971. Who should attend?

972. Who is responsible?

973. How will they be formed?

974. How effective is training that is delivered through technology-based platforms?

975. How are evaluation results utilized?

976. How do you implement Cost Reduction?

977. How is the timing of assessments organized (e.g., pre/post-test, single point during training, multiple reassessment during training)?

978. What resources do you need?

979. What happens if a team member receives a Rating of Unsatisfactory?

3.10 Issue Log: New Product And Process Development

980. Who are the members of the governing body?

981. How much time does it take to do it?

982. Is the Issue log kept In a safe place?

983. Why not more evaluators?

984. In your work, how much time is spent on stakeholder identification?

985. Who reported the issue?

986. What is the status of the issue?

987. What help do you and your team need from the stakeholders?

988. How do you reply to this question; you am new here and managing this major program. How do you suggest you build your network?

989. In classifying stakeholders, which approach to do so are you using?

990. Is there an important stakeholder who is actively opposed and will not receive messages?

991. Who is involved as you identify stakeholders?

992. Can you think of other people who might have concerns or interests?

993. How were past initiatives successful?

994. How is this initiative related to other portfolios, programs, or New Product And Process Development projects?

4.0 Monitoring and Controlling Process Group: New Product And Process Development

995. When will the New Product And Process Development project be done?

996. Is the schedule for the set products being met?

997. How well did the team follow the chosen processes?

998. Did the New Product And Process Development project team have the right skills?

999. How well defined and documented were the New Product And Process Development project management processes you chose to use?

1000. Is there sufficient time allotted between the general system design and the detailed system design phases?

1001. How well did the chosen processes produce the expected results?

1002. How is agile portfolio management done?

1003. How were collaborations developed, and how are they sustained?

1004. Who needs to be engaged upfront to ensure use of results?

1005. How was the program set-up initiated?

1006. Are there areas that need improvement?

1007. How are you doing?

1008. Who needs to be involved in the planning?

4.1 Project Performance Report: New Product And Process Development

1009. What degree are the relative importance and priority of the goals clear to all team members?

1010. To what degree does the information network communicate Information relevant to the task?

1011. To what degree will new and supplemental skills be introduced as the need is recognized?

1012. To what degree are the demands of the task compatible with and converge with the relationships of the informal organization?

1013. To what degree is there a sense that only the team can succeed?

1014. To what degree are the demands of the task compatible with and converge with the mission and functions of the formal organization?

1015. To what degree does the formal organization make use of individual resources and meet individual needs?

1016. To what degree will team members, individually and collectively, commit time to help themselves and others learn and develop skills?

1017. To what degree are the tasks requirements reflected in the flow and storage of information?

1018. To what degree are the members clear on what they are individually responsible for and what they are jointly responsible for?

1019. To what degree do team members frequently explore the teams purpose and its implications?

1020. To what degree does the informal organization make use of individual resources and meet individual needs?

1021. To what degree is there centralized control of information sharing?

1022. To what degree does the teams work approach provide opportunity for members to engage in open interaction?

1023. To what degree does the information network provide individuals with the information they require?

4.2 Variance Analysis: New Product And Process Development

1024. How are material, labor, and overhead standards set?

1025. Do work packages consist of discrete tasks which are adequately described?

1026. Is the entire contract planned in time-phased control accounts to the extent practicable?

1027. What was the cause of the increase in costs?

1028. Are procedures for variance analysis documented and consistently applied at the control account level and selected WBS and organizational levels at least monthly as a routine task?

1029. What is exceptional?

1030. Are work packages assigned to performing organizations?

1031. Are there knowledgeable New Product And Process Development projections of future performance?

1032. Are management actions taken to reduce indirect costs when there are significant adverse variances?

1033. Are estimates of costs at completion generated

in a rational, consistent manner?

1034. Budget versus actual. how does the monthly budget compare to actual experience?

1035. Are there externalities from having some customers, even if they are unprofitable in the short run?

1036. What does an unfavorable overhead volume variance mean?

1037. Is the market likely to continue to grow at this rate next year?

1038. Are records maintained to show how management reserves are used?

1039. Are the bases and rates for allocating costs from each indirect pool consistently applied?

1040. How do you evaluate the impact of schedule changes, work around, et?

1041. How does the use of a single conversion element (rather than the traditional labor and overhead elements) affect standard costing?

4.3 Earned Value Status: New Product And Process Development

1042. If earned value management (EVM) is so good in determining the true status of a New Product And Process Development project and New Product And Process Development project its completion, why is it that hardly any one uses it in Information systems related New Product And Process Development projects?

1043. When is it going to finish?

1044. Earned value can be used in almost any New Product And Process Development project situation and in almost any New Product And Process Development project environment. it may be used on large New Product And Process Development projects, medium sized New Product And Process Development projects, tiny New Product And Process Development projects (in cut-down form), complex and simple New Product And Process Development projects and in any market sector. some people, of course, know all about earned value, they have used it for years - but perhaps not as effectively as they could have?

1045. Are you hitting your New Product And Process Development projects targets?

1046. Where is evidence-based earned value in your organization reported?

1047. How much is it going to cost by the finish?

1048. Where are your problem areas?

1049. Verification is a process of ensuring that the developed system satisfies the stakeholders agreements and specifications; Are you building the product right? What do you verify?

1050. What is the unit of forecast value?

1051. How does this compare with other New Product And Process Development projects?

1052. Validation is a process of ensuring that the developed system will actually achieve the stakeholders desired outcomes; Are you building the right product? What do you validate?

4.4 Risk Audit: New Product And Process Development

1053. Are contracts reviewed before renewal?

1054. Is there a screening process that will ensure all participants have the fitness and skills required to safely participate?

1055. How do you prioritize risks?

1056. Is all expenditure authorised through an identified process?

1057. Are formal technical reviews part of this process?

1058. How do you govern assets?

1059. Can analytical tests provide evidence that is as strong as evidence from traditional substantive tests?

1060. Does your auditor understand your business?

1061. Do you have a mechanism for managing change?

1062. Will participants be required to sign a legally counselled waiver or risk disclaimer when entering an event?

1063. What are the Internal Controls ?

1064. Is the customer technically sophisticated in the product area?

1065. What can be measured?

1066. Are some people working on multiple New Product And Process Development projects?

1067. Have risks been considered with an insurance broker or provider and suitable insurance cover been arranged?

1068. To what extent are auditors influenced by the business risk assessment in the audit process, and how can auditors create more effective mental models to more fully examine contradictory evidence?

1069. From an empirical perspective, does the business risk approach lead to a more effective audit, or simply to increased consulting revenue detrimental to audit rigor?

4.5 Contractor Status Report: New Product And Process Development

1070. Are there contractual transfer concerns?

1071. How does the proposed individual meet each requirement?

1072. Describe how often regular updates are made to the proposed solution. Are corresponding regular updates included in the standard maintenance plan?

1073. What was the final actual cost?

1074. What was the overall budget or estimated cost?

1075. How long have you been using the services?

1076. How is risk transferred?

1077. If applicable; describe your standard schedule for new software version releases. Are new software version releases included in the standard maintenance plan?

1078. What process manages the contracts?

1079. What was the actual budget or estimated cost for your organizations services?

1080. What is the average response time for answering a support call?

1081. What was the budget or estimated cost for your organizations services?

1082. What are the minimum and optimal bandwidth requirements for the proposed solution?

1083. Who can list a New Product And Process Development project as organization experience, your organization or a previous employee of your organization?

4.6 Formal Acceptance: New Product And Process Development

1084. What can you do better next time?

1085. Was the client satisfied with the New Product And Process Development project results?

1086. How does your team plan to obtain formal acceptance on your New Product And Process Development project?

1087. How well did the team follow the methodology?

1088. Did the New Product And Process Development project achieve its MOV?

1089. Does it do what New Product And Process Development project team said it would?

1090. Who supplies data?

1091. General estimate of the costs and times to complete the New Product And Process Development project?

1092. Was the New Product And Process Development project managed well?

1093. Who would use it?

1094. Do you buy pre-configured systems or build your own configuration?

1095. Was the sponsor/customer satisfied?

1096. What lessons were learned about your New Product And Process Development project management methodology?

1097. What is the Acceptance Management Process?

1098. What are the requirements against which to test, Who will execute?

1099. Did the New Product And Process Development project manager and team act in a professional and ethical manner?

1100. Do you perform formal acceptance or burn-in tests?

1101. Have all comments been addressed?

1102. Does it do what client said it would?

1103. Was the New Product And Process Development project work done on time, within budget, and according to specification?

5.0 Closing Process Group: New Product And Process Development

1104. Is this an updated New Product And Process Development project Proposal Document?

1105. What is the risk of failure to your organization?

1106. Were risks identified and mitigated?

1107. What areas were overlooked on this New Product And Process Development project?

1108. Is there a clear cause and effect between the activity and the lesson learned?

1109. What were things that you need to improve?

1110. How critical is the New Product And Process Development project success to the success of your organization?

1111. Did the New Product And Process Development project team have the right skills?

1112. Were sponsors and decision makers available when needed outside regularly scheduled meetings?

1113. Is the New Product And Process Development project funded?

1114. Are there funding or time constraints?

1115. What could be done to improve the process?

1116. What is the amount of funding and what New Product And Process Development project phases are funded?

1117. Were decisions made in a timely manner?

1118. Can the lesson learned be replicated?

5.1 Procurement Audit: New Product And Process Development

1119. Did the conditions included in the contract protect the risk of non-performance by the supplier and were there no conflicting provisions?

1120. Do the buyers always select or authorize the source of supply on other than contract purchases?

1121. Were no charges billed to interested economic operators or the parties to the system?

1122. Were bids properly evaluated?

1123. Does the procurement New Product And Process Development project comply with European Communities regulations and rules?

1124. Are individuals with check-signing responsibility prohibited from signing blank checks?

1125. In case of decisions not to conclude a procurement or award a contract, were tenderers informed in writing and on a timely basis of the already stated decisions and grounds?

1126. Do procurement staff, supplier and end user communicate properly?

1127. Is there a policy on purchasing from users of organization products?

1128. Has it been determined which areas of procurement the audit should cover?

1129. Are all purchase orders accounted for?

1130. Are services/tasks combined in such a way that the market is used where relevant?

1131. Did you consider and evaluate alternatives, like bundling needs with other departments or grouping supplies in separate lots with different characteristics?

1132. Who are the key suppliers?

1133. Is there a legal authority for the procurement New Product And Process Development project?

1134. Did your organization state the minimum requirements to be met by the variants in the tender documents?

1135. Are unsuccessful companies informed why tender failed?

1136. Is there a formal program of inservice training for personnel in the business management function?

1137. Are prices always included on the purchase order?

1138. Is there a practice that prohibits signing blank purchase orders?

5.2 Contract Close-Out: New Product And Process Development

1139. How/when used ?

1140. Have all contracts been closed?

1141. Parties: Authorized?

1142. Parties: who is involved?

1143. Have all acceptance criteria been met prior to final payment to contractors?

1144. Why Outsource?

1145. How is the contracting office notified of the automatic contract close-out?

1146. Have all contracts been completed?

1147. Change in circumstances?

1148. How does it work?

1149. What is capture management?

1150. Was the contract type appropriate?

1151. Change in attitude or behavior?

1152. Have all contract records been included in the New Product And Process Development project archives?

1153. Was the contract complete without requiring numerous changes and revisions?

1154. Has each contract been audited to verify acceptance and delivery?

1155. Change in knowledge?

1156. Are the signers the authorized officials?

1157. Was the contract sufficiently clear so as not to result in numerous disputes and misunderstandings?

1158. What happens to the recipient of services?

5.3 Project or Phase Close-Out: New Product And Process Development

1159. Did the delivered product meet the specified requirements and goals of the New Product And Process Development project?

1160. What were the desired outcomes?

1161. Were the outcomes different from the already stated planned?

1162. What was learned?

1163. Complete yes or no?

1164. Who controlled the resources for the New Product And Process Development project?

1165. Is the lesson significant, valid, and applicable?

1166. What information is each stakeholder group interested in?

1167. What could have been improved?

1168. What process was planned for managing issues/risks?

1169. Who exerted influence that has positively affected or negatively impacted the New Product And Process Development project?

1170. Planned completion date?

1171. Did the New Product And Process Development project management methodology work?

1172. Were messages directly related to the release strategy or phases of the New Product And Process Development project?

1173. Was the user/client satisfied with the end product?

1174. When and how were information needs best met?

1175. Is the lesson based on actual New Product And Process Development project experience rather than on independent research?

1176. What benefits or impacts does the stakeholder group expect to obtain as a result of the New Product And Process Development project?

5.4 Lessons Learned: New Product And Process Development

1177. How efficient were New Product And Process Development project team meetings conducted?

1178. Was the schedule met?

1179. What would you change?

1180. What report generation capability is needed?

1181. What is your working hypothesis, if you have one?

1182. What is the proportion of in-house and contractor personnel authorized for the New Product And Process Development project?

1183. Was the necessary hardware, software, accommodation etc available?

1184. What is the frequency of group communications?

1185. Overall, how effective were the efforts to prepare you and your organization for the impact of the product/service of the New Product And Process Development project?

1186. How effective were the techniques used to prepare you and your organization for the impact of the changes brought about by the product or service produced by the New Product And Process Development project?

1187. What is your organizational ideology?

1188. What were the most significant issues on this New Product And Process Development project?

1189. What needs to be done over or differently?

1190. What are the expectations of the individuals?

1191. What worked well/did not work well?

1192. Where do you go from here?

1193. What was the methodology behind successful learning experiences, and how might they be applied to the broader challenge of your organizations knowledge management?

1194. What is the supplier dependency?

1195. What were the major enablers to a quick response?

Index

always 10, 260-261
ambitious   239
amended   155
amount   25, 190, 259
amplify75, 109
analysis   3, 7, 10-11, 62, 69-70, 73, 85, 89, 138, 147, 154,
172, 185, 188, 191, 204, 211, 236, 239, 248
analytical   252
analyze   2, 60, 63-64, 191
analyzed   100
analyzes   142
another   156, 165, 208
anothers   239
answer 11-12, 16, 29, 45, 60, 77, 94, 106
answered   27, 44, 59, 76, 93, 105, 131
answering   11, 167, 254
anyone   40, 117, 128
anything   143, 162, 170, 187, 230
appear   1
appetite   210
applicable   12, 100, 148, 179, 254, 264
applied   82, 101, 141, 165, 248-249, 267
appointed   34, 42
appraise   225
appreciate   198
approach   58, 85, 90, 110, 116, 155, 213, 223, 238-239, 242,
247, 253
approaches   78, 87, 201-202
approval   39, 107, 147, 237
approvals   146, 155, 182
approve   225
approved   31, 75, 151, 187, 214, 225, 227
approving   151
Architects   8
archived   187
archives   263
around108, 127, 249
arranged   253
arriving217
articulate   219
ascribed   209
asking 1, 8, 193
aspects   139, 166, 215

culture 29, 61, 197-199, 209, 236, 240
current 40, 45, 48, 55, 60, 70-71, 89, 91, 95, 106, 113, 119, 129-
130, 154, 197, 206, 213
currently   37, 116, 159, 229, 236
custom22
customer   26, 39, 43-44, 84, 95-96, 122, 124, 130, 188, 204,
207, 234, 253, 257
customers   1, 21, 35, 37, 46, 48, 51, 55, 60, 71, 95, 108, 110,
114-116, 120-121, 124-126, 129, 148, 152, 166, 189, 211, 223, 234,
249
cut-down   250
damage   1
Dashboard   9
dashboards   104
day-to-day   100, 114
deadlines   20, 113, 166
dealing   17
debriefing   215
deceitful   123
decide78, 197-198
decided   77
deciding   175
decision   6, 54, 66, 83, 86-87, 90-92, 175, 221, 229-230, 258
decisions   81-84, 86, 91, 95, 99, 105, 198, 213, 229, 234-235,
237, 259-260
dedicated   8
deeper   11
defect 181
defects   175, 191, 225, 232
define 2, 29, 73-74, 136, 178, 207, 230
defined   11-12, 16, 24, 26, 29, 31-33, 35-36, 38-43, 45, 60,
67, 77, 94, 106, 134, 145, 152-153, 155-156, 158, 160, 164, 175,
179, 182, 188-189, 192, 197, 199, 244
defines23, 35, 172
defining   8, 124, 135
definite   103, 164
definition   20, 26, 29, 39, 41, 43-44, 182, 213
degree   145, 179, 238-240, 246-247
Delaying   48, 239
delays 50, 203
delegated   43
deletions   104
deliver 21, 36, 84, 112, 122, 177, 185, 235

inherent   113, 198
in-house   266
initial   44, 180
initially 39
initiated   153, 186, 227, 245
Initiating   2, 106, 133
initiative   11, 135, 193, 219, 243
Innovate   77
innovation   45, 66, 69, 99, 116, 126, 166
innovative   110, 139, 177, 185, 221
in-process   62
inputs   32, 37, 64, 102
inservice   261
inside   21
insight 65, 70
insights 9
inspect225
inspector   225
inspired   121
Instead129
instructed   147
insurance   253
insure   123
integrate   78, 104, 127, 140, 143
integrated   207
integrity   116, 228
intended   1, 83
INTENT 16, 29, 45, 60, 77, 94, 106
intention   1
interact   130
interest129, 191, 223
interested   260, 264
interests   25, 220, 243
interfaces   155
interim 113, 240
internal   1, 40, 73, 107, 124, 154, 159, 166, 182, 191, 252
interpret   11
intervals   182
interview   120
introduce   58
introduced   246
inventory   184
invest   68

market 18, 209, 239, 249-250, 261
marketer   8
marketing   149, 155
markets   27
Maslow   174
material   159, 191, 248
Materials   1, 145
matrices   150
Matrix 3, 5, 138, 150-151, 175, 195, 209, 221
matter 40, 53, 57, 239
mature 146
maximizing   118
maximum   133
McClellan   174
McGregor   174
meaning   164
meaningful   54, 114, 238
measurable   39, 43, 133, 238
measure   2, 10, 17, 23, 31, 42, 45-46, 50, 52-58, 69, 71, 77,
79, 82, 84, 86, 88, 98, 100, 102-103, 153, 185-187, 192-193, 240
measured   19, 46-50, 52-53, 99, 102, 189, 211, 238, 253
measures   47-48, 51, 53, 55, 58, 60, 62, 69, 71, 89, 101, 191,
221, 225
measuring   158-159
mechanical   1
mechanism   225, 252
mechanisms   138
mechanized   181
medium   239, 250
meeting   31, 95, 194, 223, 236-237
meetings   34, 36, 41, 147, 182, 209, 229, 236-237, 258, 266
megatrends   110
member   6, 35, 128-129, 172, 196, 201, 223, 236, 240-241
members   41, 43, 65, 140, 160, 179, 201, 213, 234-235, 237-
240, 242, 246-247
memorable   238
mental 253
message   98
messages   201, 236, 242, 265
method   47, 192, 201, 239
methods   41, 44, 50, 71, 160, 185, 190, 209, 236
metrics 5, 31, 68, 104, 135, 154, 188, 191-192, 218
Microsoft   222

needed   16-18, 22-23, 27, 32, 64, 73-74, 95, 97, 99, 102, 144, 178, 193, 195, 199, 214, 219-220, 240, 258, 266
negative   124, 220
negatively   206, 264
negotiate   123
negotiated   110
neither 1
network   4, 168, 242, 246-247
Neutral 11, 16, 29, 45, 60, 77, 94, 106
normal 99, 191
Notice 1
noticing   229
notified   262
notifies 191
number   27, 44, 58-59, 76, 93, 105, 131, 164, 191, 236, 268
numbers   127, 175
numerous   263
objection   21, 27
objective   8, 141, 183, 209, 230
objectives   20, 25-26, 29, 33, 39, 66, 68, 104, 112, 118-119, 133, 190, 199-200, 202, 206, 223, 235, 238
observed   90
obsolete   110
obstacles   17, 177, 185
obtain 110, 214, 256, 265
obtained   43, 134, 147, 155
obviously   11
occurred   205
occurrence   225
occurring   88, 207, 219
occurs 20, 48, 95
offerings   61, 78
offerors 215
offers   216
office   217, 223, 262
officer 215
officials 263
offshore   148
one-time   8
ongoing   89, 102, 177, 231
on-going   144
opened   196
operates   115

pocket 178
pockets   178
points 27, 44, 58, 64, 76, 92, 105, 130, 138
policies   143
policy 33, 82, 97, 170, 231-232, 260
Political   36, 128
portfolio   125, 244
portfolios   243
portray 74
position   197
positioned   185-186
positive   86, 109, 124
positively   206, 264
possible   51, 54, 66, 76, 83, 94, 119, 123, 178, 181, 221, 238
post-test   241
potential   22, 63, 78, 81, 87-88, 110-111, 120, 138, 152, 202, 212
practical   66, 77, 86, 94, 224
practice   261
practices   1, 10, 63, 79, 102, 104, 142, 154, 160, 198, 222, 240
preaward   215
precaution   1
precede   168
Prediction   164, 206
predictive   172
pre-filled   9
prepare   193, 198, 266
prepared   134, 183
presence   139
present   101, 117, 122, 138, 174
presented   20, 234
presenting   233
preserve   34
preserved   67
pressures   166
prevent   52, 154, 158, 175, 216, 221
prevents   23
previous   40, 166, 179, 191, 255
previously   143, 227
priced 159
prices 216, 261
primarily   199

primary 52, 136, 160, 172
principles 141
priorities 46-47, 52-53, 57, 220
prioritize 252
priority 48, 57, 164, 195, 240, 246
privacy 33
private 141
probable 209
probably 172
problem 16, 19-21, 25-27, 29, 37-38, 40, 43, 47, 54, 64, 66, 224, 238, 251
problems 17, 19, 22, 24, 26, 85, 88, 91, 100, 122, 149, 193, 203
procedural 240
procedure 237
procedures 10, 90, 94-95, 102, 104, 144, 155, 158-159, 170, 175, 181, 188, 190-191, 213, 230, 237, 248
proceeding 178
Process 1-14, 16-44, 46-102, 104-105, 107-128, 130-138, 140-156, 158, 160-164, 166-170, 172, 174-191, 193, 195-201, 203-211, 213-217, 219, 221-225, 227, 229, 231-232, 234-236, 238-240, 242-244, 246, 248, 250-262, 264-267
processes 48, 55, 61-63, 66-69, 73-74, 96, 99, 104, 134, 140, 154-155, 161, 175, 226-227, 237, 244
produce 64, 141, 170, 223, 244
produced 61, 86, 153, 267
producing 150, 232
Product 1-14, 16-44, 46-93, 95-102, 104-105, 107-128, 130-138, 140-148, 150-156, 158, 160-164, 166-170, 172, 174-191, 193, 195-201, 203-211, 213-217, 219, 221-225, 227-229, 231, 234-236, 238, 240, 242-244, 246, 248, 250-262, 264-267
production 36, 89, 114, 133, 237
products 1, 18, 21, 108, 116, 141, 150, 183, 191, 207, 223, 228, 244, 260
profile 206
program 20, 69, 96, 140-142, 144, 203, 221, 242, 245, 261
programme 222
programs 141, 143, 224, 226, 243
progress 42, 48, 84, 104, 112, 115, 153-154, 186, 193-194, 213, 222, 236, 240
prohibited 260
prohibits 261

Lightning Source UK Ltd.
Milton Keynes UK
UKHW021307070620
364499UK00002B/133

9 781867 405955